Calvin B. Rock

Go
On!

Vital Messages
for Today's
Christian

REVIEW AND HERALD® PUBLISHING ASSOCIATION
HAGERSTOWN, MD 21740

The author assumes full responsibility for the accuracy of all facts and
quotations as cited in this book.

This book was
Edited by Gerald Wheeler
Designed by Patricia S. Wegh
Cover design by Willie Duke
Cover photo by Joel D. Springer
Typeset: 12/14 Weiss

PRINTED IN U.S.A.

98 97 96 95 94   10 9 8 7 6 5 4 3 2 1

R&H Cataloging Service
Rock, Calvin B.
    Go on!

    1. Oakwood College.   2. Sermons—Seventh-day
Adventist.   3. Afro-American Seventh-day Adventists—
Sermons.   I. Title.

        252.086732

ISBN 0-8280-0815-9

PREFACE

$t$he chapters of this volume are the condensed expression of 14 years of Sabbath sermons given at Oakwood College. Of course, I shared many other presentations with the college community. A few of them I have reproduced in various books and journals—and others I rightfully relegated to obscurity.

Thomas Wolfe was correct: "You can't go home again." Our present is really the future flowing swiftly into the ever-receding past. We cannot freeze the frames and cling to the good we would cherish. However, we can retain meaningful thought and allow it to strengthen us for present challenges.

My sincere hope is that those who were helped by these talks will be blessed again, and that the considerable number of students who chided me for presenting messages that they regarded as too stilted will have grown sufficiently to hear them seriously now. On the other hand, I frankly confess to having shortened them in a needed, if belated, effort to make them less pedantic and, certainly, less ponderous.

As you will observe, the connecting thread of these talks is an attempt to awaken and nurture faith in God and His people. I did this under the firm conviction that the audience to whom I spoke had been targeted in a special way to fulfill Paul's promise: "They without us should not be made perfect" (Heb. 11:40). While that may have been too sanguine a hope, the joy and excitement of seeing so many youth express and exercise commitment to Christian service is reward enough.

These messages provide an up-close look into the challenges presented the Oakwood campus family during a very narrow slice of history. They will, I hope, inspire all who retrace this journey to increased holiness and a more joyful expression of the blessed hope.

FOREWORD

I'm extremely excited to have the privilege of writing this foreword for Dr. Calvin B. Rock's latest literary presentation—a collection of his masterful sermons. Not only was he one of my most admired expositors of the Word and a model of a minister for me, but he was president of Oakwood College, my alma mater, and my president on my first job after graduation at the college.

Dr. Rock is noted for many things, but the one event that remains freshest in the mind of Oakwood College graduates during his tenure is his challenge at every graduation ceremony. After the address, after the class response, after the singing of the college song, after receiving the diploma and changing the tassel, then Dr. Rock would stand up to challenge the graduating class in his customary two-word, five-minute speech. Spoken with cadence, and fervency, inspired with tradition, Rock would declare, "Go, go on, go on. Go on, go on. Go on, go on, go on, . . ." And on and on until the room rocked with rhythm and elation. From this inspiration graduates would depart to achieve new heights of personal and professional growth.

Once again Dr. Rock enraptures me with his gift for profoundness with God's Word. And as I reviewed this small but powerful presentation, chapters like "The Paradoxes of Success" and "I Am Joseph" renewed within me the richness and deep spirituality of Rock's preaching. I can still see him standing tall and stately, leaning slightly forward in the pulpit, his right hand raised, his index finger extended and keeping pace with his prophetic and heartfelt utterances. I can still hear the cadence, the urgency, the ardency, the pathos, in his voice as he fastens upon each powerful point of his message, explaining and urging application of God's Word. If you were there, you were blessed. If you were there, you remember.

Calvin B. Rock has captured part of the inspiration of his Oakwood years of preaching and encapsuled it within the pages of this book, which is interestingly titled *Go On!* And irrespective of whether you have had the "Oakwood experience" or not, through these sermons he still appeals to readers to "Go on" to new heights of spiritual growth, "Go on" to new levels of personal development, "Go on" to new realms of excellence, "Go on" to a deeper, richer relationship and experience with Christ, "Go on" until we are at last graduated to be with Him in eternity.

Steve Ruff, editor
Message magazine

CONTENTS

Chapter 1

WE ARE DEBTORS —AND THAT'S FOR SURE

"I am a debtor both to the Greeks, and to the Barbarians; both to the wise, and to the unwise. So, as much as in me is, I am ready to preach the gospel to you that are at Rome also" (Rom. 1:14, 15).

One of the more arresting characteristics of Paul's epistles is the imagery he uses to describe himself. In Romans he introduces himself as a *servant* of Jesus Christ (Rom. 1:1); in Corinthians he is an *apostle* of Jesus Christ (1 Cor. 1:1) and a *fool* in glorying in Christ (2 Cor. 12:11); in Ephesians he labels himself a *prisoner* for Christ (Eph. 3:1); and in 1 Timothy he refers to himself as the *chief of sinners* (1 Tim. 1:15).

Each self-portrait of his discipleship has rich meaning. However, what expresses perhaps more than anything else the essence of his dedication is the analogy in Romans 1:14, where he declares himself to be Paul, the *debtor*. Here he portrays his services as that of one under obligation to God and humanity because of heaven's mercies. And for God's great gifts he pledges to pay "as much as in me is" for the rest of his life.

Paul's "debtor motif" is a valid model for Christians of all ages. Its meaning is as clear to our business-oriented society as it was to the trade-centered generation in which he lived.

We moderns know well the dynamics of debt. We borrow to establish credit and we borrow to keep that credit. Ironically, we borrow to pay our bills, and by doing so, we make more bills; we borrow because it is convenient, we borrow because it's fashionable, we borrow because we must. Our society is deep in debt—personally, corporately, regionally, and nationally. Indebtedness is an ingrained part of our culture and, as such, a relevant and apt description of our discipleship.

Consider the many aspects of our moral indebtedness: We are first of all indebted to *nature*. Born in sin, we are all, through no choosing of our own, among "the living [who] know that they shall die." Death is an inescapable fact of human reality.

Go On!

We are all candidates for nonbeing. Although we do not know when the journey will end, we do know that a grave awaits us at the end of the road. The divine decree—"dust to dust"—hangs like a cosmic cloud over all of us. Even as Adam lived 930 years "and he died," so shall we.

Oh, yes, belief in the Second Coming gives us hope of escaping death. But for those of us who have moved through youth into middle and old age, and even for you who follow hard upon our heels, grim reality means faith in the resurrection as well as translation. Although we still hope for the Apocalypse, meanwhile if we are wise we update our wills, we pay our life insurance, and even select retirement locations and burial plots.

And the older we grow, the more we understand what the prophet meant when she said, "The human family have scarcely begun to live when they begin to die" (*Christ's Object Lessons*, p. 342). And the advance of age helps us to resonate with the poet when he wrote, "Life is real! Life is earnest! . . . And our hearts, though stout and brave, still, like muffled drums, are beating funeral marches to the grave" (Longfellow, "A Psalm of Life").

The truth is that our classmates and loved ones who have preceded us in death have paid an obligation that we too must someday render. Time and nature will surely exact their just compensation. Should time last, death is an obligation we will not escape—we are debtors, and that's for sure!

Second, we are debtors to *transgression*. Every breach of law carries its penalty. Thus our indebtedness to nature includes not only the death that follows life but also the scars of sin that mar our living. Forgiveness of our sins does not cancel the suffering they have caused. The law of cause and effect imposes its irrevocable consequences upon us long before we die. Every breach of the law of God affects our bodies, our minds and/or emotions, and our intellect. The decline of our bodies and the emotional disintegration of our psychological selves are sure consequences of our sins.

But we pay in more ways than these. We pay in the moral breakdown of our race, in the spiritual decadence of our institutions, and even in the mistakes and misdirections of our posterity.

Because as adolescents we dipped into the capital of our later years, spending ahead on the vital energies of life, and because we still sometimes mortgage the future for present goals—working too hard, exercising too little, and eating too much—we suffer. Yes, sin is slaying us all, working its daily concupiscence within (Rom. 7:8). We are debtors, and that's for sure!

But then we are also debtors in a positive sense—debtors, that is, to a long list

10

of courageous men and women whose sacrifices have purchased our political and social freedoms.

We Blacks did not arrive unaided at our present socio-economic level. We are Black, and for the past several centuries that—especially in the Western world—has been a symbol of inferiority—the sign of a curse.

It is not perfect in America, but the fact that we are no longer consigned to the back of the bus, the top of the theater, the side of the cafeteria, the front of the train, and the bottom of the boat is testimony to the efforts of many selfless individuals.

True, we are not yet equal in income, opportunity, or power. Human perfidy and the tyranny of numbers prevent that. But we are a long way from the terrors of slavery and the indignities of Reconstruction, and to that we are in debt.

The people who bought our freedom were a diversified lot—some White, some Black, some rich and famous, some poor and unheralded—but each in his or her own way helped to create the atmosphere and to establish the laws that have allowed our education, bought our houses, elected us in Alabama politics, bathed us on Texas beaches, fed us in Carolina cafeterias, slept us in Mississippi motels, and buried us in Arlington Cemetery. And we are debtors for all that.

We are debtors to George Fox, the Quaker leader who in 1688 led the first public protest against slavery. We are indebted to John Brown, who died fighting superior odds in an attempt to overthrow slave rule, and we are indebted to Henry Clay for his fiery Congressional speeches. We are indebted to Gabriel Prosser, the Black Samson; to Denmark Vesey, the Black Joshua; and to Nat Turner—all of whom were rebel slaves who could "take no more," and each of whom was hanged after leading insurrections for freedom.

And we are indebted to Richard Allen, the Black Methodist who left the balcony to pray on the main floor and, when expelled from the Methodist Episcopal Church, established the African Methodist Episcopal Church.

We are indebted to Harriet Tubman and to all the other conductors of the Underground Railroad. We are indebted to Crispus Attucks, to Sojourner Truth, to William DeBuis, to Frederick Douglass, to Marcus Garvey, to Dory Miller, to Paul Robeson, to Adam Clayton Powell, to Rosa Parks, to John F. Kennedy, to Robert Kennedy, to Lyndon Baines Johnson, to Thurgood Marshall, to Martin Luther King, Jr., and to Jimmy Carter. They risked, they suffered, and many died that we might be free.

It is by their contribution that our pockets are lined, our pantries are filled, our streets have been paved, and our CD's bear interest. They are our material and moral benefactors, their sacrifices dwarf our meager courage and shame our selfish hoardings. We are debtors, and that's for sure!

And can anyone doubt that we are also debtors to the church—to the Christian church in general? We are indebted to Christianity because it stitched together our families after slavery ripped them apart. It gave us material support during economic recessions and depressions. The study of its Bible brought us literacy, and its churches provided most of the champions of our civil rights.

And in particular we here owe a debt to the Seventh-day Adventist Church. It taught us how to tithe, and that raised the level of our affluence. It brought us the Sabbath, and that gave us social cohesion. Adventism offered us health reform and that increased our longevity, and it exposed us to dress reform and that aided our dignity and identity as a special people.

Seventh-day Adventism taught us the state of the dead, freeing us from superstition and witchcraft. It gave us Christian education, not only shaping our distinctive worldview but also providing us with tools for service, and the special camaraderie that binds us to our origins and to one another.

We are indebted to Ellen White, who articulated all these principles so clearly; to J. O. Corliss, who first preached to the Blacks in the South; to James Edson White, who built the boat that traveled down the Mississippi; and to G. E. Peters, who helped hold our people in the faith when men as bright and as charismatic as he were leaving the church and inviting us to join them.

We are indebted to J. H. Waggoner for the vision and energy to launch Pine Forge, to J. L. Moran for his work during the transition years at Oakwood, to N. C. Druillard for the inspiration of Riverside Hospital, to L. B. Reynolds for elevating *Message* magazine, to E. E. Cleveland for revolutionizing our evangelism, and to Rosa Banks for demonstrating that females can indeed contribute with effectiveness at the highest levels of church authority.

We've come a long way from Charles Bowles to Charles Bradford. And our church is chiefly responsible for our advances. While its record is not perfect—it has not done all that it should—it has done more than anybody else. For that, we are debtors, and that's for sure!

And, as executors of Christ's will we are debtors to the totality of humanity. An executor is one chosen by the "will maker" to inform all recipients of the will their inheritance.

The executor sees that the news of inheritance reaches all those who are beneficiaries. That is what Paul meant when he said, "I am debtor both to the Greeks, and to the Barbarians; both to the wise, and the unwise."

We Are Debtors—And That's for Sure

The apostle saw the lostness of humanity, he knew the vanity of Grecian wisdom, the depravity of Barbarian ritual, and the deception of Roman might. He knew that human wisdom and might was finite and fleeting, and its final end destruction.

Having been rescued from the kingdom of darkness by his loving Lord—he saw himself called to share with all the excitement of the Master's will—the good news that as heirs of God and joint heirs with Christ, each may receive mercies far exceeding any earthly possession.

And it's not just news of "pie in the sky, way by and by" that we preach. It's also "food on the plate while we wait."

In the Master's will we have joy that money cannot buy, peace that knowledge cannot bring, faith that riches do not procure, and love that wealth will not produce.

But it's not all emotional compensation, either. The Master's will offers the presence of angels pledged to protect us; the comforts of goodness and mercy delegated to follow us; the promise that our bread and water will never fail; the assurance that all things work together for good to them that love the Lord; and Christ's righteous robe to cover our imperfections. We are debtors, and that's for sure!

Those of us who have found the Messiah owe it to our neighbors and kin to tell them about Him. Either we do it or they will die wealthy beggars, affluent paupers, included by Christ's love but excluded by our indolence. They will live and die—if we do not tell them—Christless and condemned. To them we are debtors, and that's for sure!

If the truth be told, our task is beyond our abilities. We do not have the wherewithal to repay our heroic ancestors, nor do we have the natural resources to reach the multitudes so tightly bound in materialism, rationalism, pleasurism, and all the other ideologies of death.

How can we pay when our capital is so small and the debt is so large?

There is only one way—and that is to surrender our lives in total sacrifice to God's cause, or, to paraphrase the apostle, we shall pay "as much as in us is." We can never adequately pay, but we can—and we must—spend our lives in faithfully dispensing the Master's goods.

This then is the greatest debt of all. We owe Christ not simply as a borrower does a banker or an executor to an inheritor, but as a slave owes a master, as a servant a king, or as a soldier his country—we owe Him our lives!

We owe Him for Bethlehem, where divinity combined with humanity to solve salvation's riddle. We own Him for Gethsemane—where love and resolution overcame rejection and the fear of death. We owe Him for Calvary—where His righteous blood activated the cash register of heaven, ejecting a love receipt marked "Paid in full."

And we will owe Him on the other side, for even though we pay the penalty of death, we have escaped its ultimate grasp and we shall "rise again." Casting our crowns down at His pierced feet we shall there proclaim, "Worthy is the Lamb that was slain to receive power, and riches, and wisdom, and strength, and honour, and glory" (Rev. 5:12).

There immortal, incorruptible, and glorified, our superior perceptions will but heighten our capacity to conceive His redemptive acts and more clearly know the wondrous, everlasting truth that "we are debtors—and that's for sure!"

Chapter 2

THE VIOLENCE OF DISCIPLESHIP

"And from the days of John the Baptist until now the kingdom of heaven suffereth violence, and the violent take it by force" (Matt. 11:12).

"Violence" is a frightening word. It conjures up repulsive images.

And yet we notice that twice in this one brief verse Jesus elevates violence as a virtue of discipleship, extolling it as both natural and necessary to salvation. That certainly doesn't sound like Jesus, does it?

Just a few days earlier He had said, "Love your enemies, bless those who curse you" (Matt. 5:43, NKJV). If someone slaps you on one side of the face, "turn to him the other also" (verse 39).

And in that same discussion He had said: "In the old days it was ruled: 'an eye for an eye and a tooth for a tooth.' But I say unto you that if they grab you and take away your coat, give them your sweater also, and if they demand that you go one mile, go two" (see verses 38, 40, 41).

"Blessed are the poor in spirit," He had said. And "blessed are the meek" and "blessed are the peacemakers." How then can He advocate violence as necessary in His kingdom, advising that only violent individuals can successfully negotiate its terms?

Could this really be Jesus? He sounds like a radical or terrorist who hijacks planes or kidnaps diplomats. His words fit better our concept of an enraged zealot who butchers helpless villagers in some faraway civil or tribal war.

They are the people we connect with violence—not Jesus.

Did not Isaiah prophesy that He would do no violence (Isa. 53:9)? And yet here He is advocating it as an authentic Christian characteristic. How do we explain this? What could He possibly mean?

Our search for answers starts by noticing that the kingdom Jesus refers to in this verse is not the kingdom of glory to be established when He returns. It is not the *everlasting* kingdom for which we petition when we pray "Thy kingdom come,

Thy will be done."

Rather it is the kingdom of grace portrayed earlier in Matthew 4:17: "From that time Jesus began to preach, and to say, Repent: for the kingdom of heaven is at hand."

That this kingdom differs from the physical "kingdom to come" is clear from Christ's words regarding John the Baptist: "Notwithstanding he that is least in the kingdom of heaven is greater than he" (Matt. 11:11).

Because John, then in prison, would not live to witness the glories of the kingdom of *grace*—the lowliest child who witnessed His ministry had infinite advantage by comparison.

On the other hand, the violence John suffered is not unlike the pain every participant in the grace-kingdom must endure.

"My kingdom," Jesus is saying, "is a principle that is guaranteed to cause pain. When the gospel hits home, it comes with violent impact." When it strikes, it hurts. It smashes our pride and sears our egos. We feel the pangs of withdrawal and the hurt of separation as our darling sins melt away before the white-hot heat of trials.

The kingdom of grace does come violently—it pulls away at our pet indulgences, it pries loose our preconceived traditions, and it wrestles from our grasp our cherished conceptions. It exposes the folly of traditions and meaningless superstitions, it reorders our priorities, rearranges our diets, restructures our friendships, redirects our interests, and shuts down long-standing associations. The kingdom demands painful separation from past alliances.

When the kingdom strikes, it is sometimes necessary to change jobs, schools, and even addresses. It makes a stiff impact and reorders violently.

At times it separates husbands from wives, and parents from children, as when "two women shall be grinding at the mill; the one shall be taken, and the other left" (Matt. 24:41).

It grates away like the jeweler's wheel on the rough texture of our unfinished characters, cutting away the jagged edges until we are left polished and shining.

To prepare us for the kingdom of glory, Christ must first embellish us in the kingdom of grace. The process calls for sacrifice and change! And that is what Jesus meant when He said, "The kingdom of heaven suffereth violence."

But the word "suffereth" has yet another focus. For the kingdom not only strikes violently, it attracts hostilities wherever it goes. Christ emphasized this fact when He said: "Think not that I am come to send peace on earth: I came not to send peace, but a sword" (Matt. 10:34).

Paul reinforced the same thought when he wrote, "All that will live godly in

Christ Jesus shall suffer persecution" (2 Tim. 3:12).

Again, John the Baptist's situation was symbolic. At the very moment of Christ's conversation, John's enemies were plotting his death. Before long he would be beheaded. The Baptist saw the ominous shadow of his demise creeping across his prison bars, and he did not understand it.

He sent his disciples to ask Christ, "Art thou he that should come, or do we look for another?" (Matt. 11:3).

Christ ordered John's disciples to tell him of the miracles they had witnessed—of the blind that saw, the lame that walked, and the dead that were raised, but also that Satan was contesting Christ's intrusion into his territory, and that this would make the kingdom of grace a realm of pain and violence.

And so it has always been. Not only did John the Baptist experience violence, but so did John the revelator, Stephen, Peter, James, Paul, and apparently all of Christ's early followers.

And it has continued all through the centuries. Christian believers in every era have suffered and died for their faith—some, like their Lord, nailed to crosses, others burned alive, stoned, fed to starving beasts, poisoned, drowned, and even buried alive.

The history of the church poignantly fulfills our Lord's sobering prediction of suffering for His cause.

Even where physical suffering is not great the violence of materialism and the tyranny of prosperity bring pain and grief to God's people. Yes, even here today—the kingdom of heaven suffereth violence!

Ironically, however, our primary sufferings are not occasioned by violence from without, but from dissension within. Our greatest enemy is us! And our deepest wounds are self-inflicted—initiated by the pride that fuels our bickering, complaining, the friendly fire of our evil surmisings.

The cannibalizing we practice at Sabbath dinner is more lethal to our spirituality than any hostile society. It is not only to the hatred from without but to the animosity within that Jesus refers when He said, "The kingdom of heaven suffereth violence."

Thus Christ sought to prepare both John's disciples and His own for the inevitable. "My operations," He warned, "are no piece of cake, no namby-pamby program. This is no social club. This is not a society for the passive and fearful. It is no journey for the fainthearted, no ride for wimps. This is a bloody, painful, difficult operation. You must strap on your electric chair and follow Me. Before the crown comes the cross.

"There is no other way—the kingdom of heaven suffereth violence!"

Go On!

But not only is it true that the kingdom of heaven strikes violently and in turn is violently received; it is also a fact that only the violent can endure its terms. Or, in the language of Christ: "The violent take it by force."

The Amplified Bible has it: "And from the days of John the Baptist until the present time the kingdom of heaven has endured violent assault . . . —a share in the heavenly kingdom is sought for with most ardent zeal and intense exertion" (Matt. 11:12).

In other words, only those who pursue salvation with painful determination are eligible for eternal life. Only those who yield all and risk all receive salvation.

No, we do not work our way to heaven. Romans 3 and 4, Galatians 5, and Isaiah 61:10, among other Bible passages, make it clear that it is Christ's righteousness that qualifies us for everlasting life.

We can never merit salvation. No amount of trying gains us acceptance in the glory kingdom.

But that does not negate trying. Everlasting rewards await those who strive (Luke 13:24), endure (Matt. 10:22), fight (1 Tim. 6:12), wrestle (Eph. 6:12), press on (Phil. 3:14), resist (James 4:7), and who, having done all to stand—stand! (Eph. 6:13, 14).

As I attended the Olympics in Los Angeles, I watched athletes from all over the world compete for prizes and national honor. I saw them run, jump, and throw with dedicated effort.

To me, the most awesome sight was that of the women sprinters fiercely competing against each other. You'll pardon my nationalism and my racial pride, but the group I most wanted to win were the Americans and particularly the Black men and women from the United States. I confess to having had special hopes for their success.

As they stretched their muscles and crouched down in their starting blocks, I peered through my binoculars, anticipating the pop of the starter's gun.

I held my breath as the starter's pistol fired, and they bolted from their positions and started around the track. And as they ran, these heroes from the ghetto competing against the rest of the world, I saw other scenes. I saw their ancestors dragged out of Africa and piled into slave ships and transported across an unfriendly ocean.

I remembered how the slavers threw the sick and disabled overboard—one third of this human cargo by some accounts—before dumping the rest upon our shores. I thought of the auction blocks, of the suffering, the misery, and the abuse that these runners' forebears had endured, and of the ignominy and second-class citizenship that the race has suffered since. "Oh God, it isn't much," I prayed, "but here's a chance to bring dignity and a sense of self-worth to a class of people who desperately need it." And my heart cried out, "Run, my people, run."

The Violence of Discipleship

And I saw them do just that—their veins and sinews straining with effort. They had trained and sacrificed for years. Their preparation had been violent, and so was their performance. And for the most part, they were victors. As I witnessed their successes, I cried. I wept for all their suffering ancestors, for them, for their nation, for their race, and for all those martyrs who made their successes possible. A sense of national and family pride overwhelmed me.

The life of Christ is our greatest example of violent overcoming. The Incarnation was a mysterious and violent process. At His birth Herod violently sought Him. In the wilderness Satan violently tempted Him. All through His life He faced violent opposition. In fact, "Satan contested every inch of ground, exerting his utmost power to overcome Him" (Ellen G. White, "God's Justice and Love," *Signs of the Times*, Aug. 27, 1902). The weight of His mission violently pressed down on Him in Gethsemane. During His trials priests, people, and potentates violently abused Him. Finally He was violently nailed to the cross and was then "lifted by several powerful men and thrust with great violence into the place prepared for it, causing the most excruciating agony" (*The Story of Redemption*, p. 222).

Christ's call to discipleship today includes a similar commitment to service. His cause demands absolute dedication, the consecration of all to the will of God.

Violent surrender has been the mark of true discipleship in all ages.

Abraham, who obeyed all of God's commands with respect to Isaac, was a violent believer. Jacob, who expended all his energies in grappling with the angel, was a violent confessor. Esther, who hazarded all before the king, was a violent petitioner. The farmer who sold all to acquire the treasure-filled land was a violent investor. The widow who contributed all to the Temple coffers was a violent giver. The woman at the well who told about Christ was a violent proclaimer. The woman of the crowd who ignored all and touched the hem of His garment was a violent pursuer. Jesus, who left all, was tempted in all, suffered all, forgave all, and conquered all, demands no less a surrender from us.

Chapter 3

IF I SHOULD WAKE
BEFORE I DIE

"Why all this stress on behavior? Because, as I think you have realised, the present time is of the highest importance—it is time to wake up to reality. Every day brings God's salvation nearer" (Rom. 13:11, Phillips).

Bet you can't say the Lord's prayer!"

"Sure, I can. 'Now I lay me down to sleep; I pray the Lord my soul to keep. If I should die before I wake, I pray the Lord my soul to take.'"

"Wow! I didn't really think you could do it."

Thus went the conversation between two well-meaning but misinformed teenagers on a big city playground—or so the story goes.

Of course, the real tragedy is not that so many children use this jingle in prayer, but that so many grown people order their daily lives by its meaning. True, many may address God in more sophisticated language, but they never outgrow the thrust of this simplistic chant, and cruise through life half awake/half asleep.

Their actions seem to say, "Lord, I really don't know where I am going, or how I am going to get there. I know I haven't put it together yet. I realize that my outlook is rather fuzzy and that things aren't going so well, but if judgment catches me out here and things haven't worked out quite right, please, Jesus, save me anyway."

I'd like to suggest that our real concern should be not whether we "die before we wake." What ought to challenge us is whether we shall "wake before we die"!

What does it mean to wake before we die? It means putting together a clear-cut philosophy of living and matching that creed with a practical, healthy, productive lifestyle. It means consciously embracing particular goals and setting healthy priorities. It means zeroing in on the fundamental laws of the moral universe and employing those principles in one's daily experience.

Such an outlook includes a number of critical concerns. First and foremost is the realization of *the sacredness of time.* Ellen White puts it this way:

If I Should Wake Before I Die

"Our time belongs to God. Every moment is His, and we are under the most solemn obligation to improve it to His glory. Of no talent He has given will He require a more strict account than of our time.

"The value of time is beyond computation. Christ regarded every moment as precious, and it is thus that we should regard it. Life is too short to be trifled away" (*Christ's Object Lessons*, p. 342).

Some panic at these words and drive body and mind to intemperate one-sided excess. I have no patience with such extremes. We should live like the seasons—with regularity but also with variety. The point is, however, that most people live closer to the evil of too little than they do the crime of too much. For such the challenge is not dying before they wake but waking before they die.

The second understanding implied in this concept is *the high cost of excellence.* Moffatt interprets Proverbs 22:29: "You see a man skilful at his work? He shall enter the service of kings, not the service of obscure men."

More than any other factor, hard work separates the dreamers from the achievers.

Thomas Edison expressed the thought most aptly when he said that genius is 1 percent inspiration and 99 percent perspiration.

Speaking of what it took to develop his skills, Alexander Hamilton said, "All of the genius I have is merely the fruit of labor."

Thomas Carlyle declared, "Genius is an infinite capacity for taking pains."

Ted Williams, Boston's Splendid Splinter, elected to baseball's Hall of Fame and believed by many authorities to be the greatest hitting stylist in baseball history, was not born that way. Those who know him best call him a dedicated perfectionist. What made him rise above the herd was an insatiable curiosity about all aspects of hitting a baseball and his constant efforts to improve himself.

Willie Hoppe, with a dedication worthy of more noble endeavors, developed an array of unbelievable skills in his sport and is arguably billiard king of all time. In explaining how he did it, he said, "I went to bed early. And I practiced five or six hours every day of my life."

Carol Heiss, when but a girl of 18, became the world's champion figure skater. How did she do it? By practicing four hours a day for 11 months a year.

The epitaph over many a wasted life might well read: "No deposit, no return!" Listen again to the prophet:

"God does not bid the youth to be less aspiring. The elements of character that make a man successful and honored among men—the irrepressible desire for some greater good, the indomitable will, the strenuous exertion, the untiring perseverance—are not to be crushed out" (*Messages to Young People*, p. 25).

So dream, my young friend, but remember: "Luck is preparation meeting opportunity," and furthermore, "you can get run over even in the right road if you just sit there." The only way to make dreams come true is to "wake before you die."

The third implied element of success is *the thrill of knowledge*. Random House defines knowledge as (1) acquaintance with facts, truths, or principles as from study or investigation, and (2) familiarity with a particular subject.

I believe that next to conversion, acquiring knowledge is life's most satisfying experience. It is an awesomely wonderful thing to take a mind limited in scope and expand and widen its perception.

For the primitive, there are no such things as Concorde jets, televisions, microwave ovens, and laser medicine. They exist, but not for him or her. But when discovered, they open a whole new world of aesthetic and utilitarian joy.

We might all survive (after all, a lot of other people did!) believing the world is flat, but it is much more illuminating to discover that it is 25,000 miles in circumference, 8,000 miles in diameter, tilted at about 23 degrees, and rotating at the rate of 18.5 miles per second.

It is all right to look at the stars and say, "Wow, aren't they pretty?" but it is much more meaningful to be able to pick out the Milky Way, the Big Dipper, or Orion, and to know that the human eye can see 7,000 stars, 50,000 through field glasses, and billions through telescopes.

It is all right to exclaim that our bodies are fearfully and wonderfully made, but it is truly exciting to learn that our heart beats 100,000 times a day, that our blood travels 12,000 miles every minute, and that our ears have 24,000 microscopic hair cells to catch sound waves with.

It's all right to look at springtime butterflies and marvel at their scintillating hues, but it is another thing to know that 110,000 varieties of butterflies inhabit North America—each with its own distinctive color and characteristics.

The chief value of all this is not just that it gives us accurate information about our complex universe, but that it points us to our great God and Creator. That is why the wise man advised:

"My son, if thou wilt receive my words, and hide my commandments with thee; so that thou incline thine ear unto wisdom, and apply thine heart to understanding; yea, if thou criest after knowledge, and liftest up thy voice for understanding; if thou seekest her as silver, and searchest for her as for hid treasures; then shalt thou understand the fear of the Lord, and find the knowledge of God" (Prov. 2:1-5).

If I Should Wake Before I Die

How tragic then to dabble in the mudholes of ignorance on life's vast beaches when we could be plunging into the deep waters of wisdom, reveling in the arts, sciences, and humanities, stretching the mind, and expanding our abilities to both appreciate our God and to help others. If only we could wake before we die!

A fourth primary factor involved in our approach is the *value of self-respect.* By that I do not mean a nervous concern about what others think of us, but rather a regard for personal dignity, nobility, and refinement.

Now, I think that I am somewhat in tune with the younger generation's disdain for the meaningless traditions and ceremonies of their elders. I share their dislike for phonies, for plastic people, and for the "joyful robots" of our copycat society.

I resonate with that element of the cultural revolution that refuses to accept "business as usual" in the face of the inequities of our depersonalized society. Some of us parents, believe it or not, also deplore the wastefulness of our bankrupt bureaucracy.

But what I cannot see and refuse to accept is a wholesale rejection of restraint and standard values. Is there nothing worth preserving? Must we go from a state of selfish technocracy to what Kant calls a "state of nature"—a culture of anarchy without rules and systems?

I hear the youth of our Black communities crying "nation time." But I ask you, is that a call to self-reliance and dignity, or is it an excuse to act any way they want? To let it all hang out—both our dangling participles and our undershirts?

Is it "nation time" when we play records so loudly that roommates and dormmates find it impossible to study? Is it nation time when we park where the signs say not to, when we pilfer books from the college library, when we race cars over the campus roads or wear hats while eating in the cafeteria? Well, if it is, I wish to declare myself a "noncitizen," and wonder how it would be for us and for our people if we would exercise our freedoms by respecting others, by caring for our environment, and by seeking personal growth. If only we could wake before we die!

Finally, may I encourage you to awaken and behold the *secret of holiness.*

Why is it that we who possess such a dynamite gospel live such firecracker lives? Is it because we do not follow the equation of holiness?

The equation?

It is very simple: SD + SO = SV. That is, a Strong Defense + a Strong Offense = Sure Victory.

What do I mean by defense? Prohibiting anything from dulling our five senses, thus weakening our souls. Posting No Trespassing signs to evil and refusing to keep company with whatever is destructive to our spiritual experience.

Go On!

What is the offensive component of our equation?

It is active participation in anything that strengthens resolve and charges our spiritual batteries—prayer (personal, family, and public), Bible study, fasting, and personal witness.

Contrary to what some football coaches teach, the best defense is indeed a good offense. Our prophet said it well: "The best way to prevent the growth of evil is to preoccupy the soil" (*Messages to Young People*, p. 282).

Thus, my teammates in God's Word become a wall of protection about me. I turn to them for comfort and strength, and they never fail in their assignments.

At center I have this little fellow Jude, who peers over the ball and shouts before each temptation, "Now unto him that is able to keep you from falling . . ."

My two ends are knowledgable veterans of combat. At the right Peter reminds me, "Gird up the loins of your mind, be sober, and hope to the end" (1 Peter 1:13). And on the left Paul says, "God is faithful, who will not suffer you to be tempted above that ye are able; but will with the temptation also make a way to escape" (1 Cor. 10:13).

My guards are James and John. James states, "Resist the devil, and he will flee" (James 4:7). And John declares, "My little children, these things write I unto you that ye sin not. And if any man sin, we have an advocate with the Father, Jesus Christ the righteous" (1 John 2:1).

The tackles are those giants of the Old Testament, Isaiah and David. On every play Isaiah rears his massive hulk and cries, "This is the way, walk ye in it" (Isa. 30:21). And often I hear David shouting, "Surely he shall deliver thee from the snare of the fowler, and from the noisome pestilence. He shall cover thee with his feathers, and under his wings shalt thou trust" (Ps. 91:3, 4).

My blocking back is Moses, who urges, "Be strong and of a good courage, fear not, nor be afraid of them: for the Lord thy God, he it is that doth go with thee; he will not fail thee, nor forsake thee" (Deut. 31:6).

The flanker is Solomon, who signals, "Trust in the Lord with all thine heart; and lean not unto thine own understanding. In all thy ways acknowledge him, and he shall direct thy paths" (Prov. 3:5, 6).

And my quarterback is Jesus. He hands me the ball and says, "Take up your cross and follow Me!"

With such protection and encouragement we can enthusiastically run to righteousness. Such insights will enable us to plan and execute the boldest of dreams. We can now paraphrase and pray:

If I Should Wake Before I Die

Now I rise and face my day,
I give Thee, Lord, my will and way.
If I should wake before I die,
Oh, how my joys would multiply.

Chapter 4

OCCUPY TILL I COME

"He said therefore, A certain nobleman went into a far country to receive for himself a kingdom, and to return. And he called his ten servants, and delivered them ten pounds, and said unto them, Occupy till I come" (Luke 19:12, 13).

*t*he expression "Occupy till I come" has come upon hard times. It is one of those misused injunctions usually twisted to rationalize our excesses—or more frankly, to excuse our disobedience.

As a theological loophole, "Occupy till I come" ranks right up there with "The ox is in the ditch," "When in Rome do as the Romans do," and "Be ye therefore wise as serpents, and harmless as doves" (Matt. 10:16).

All these expressions deserve better usage than they generally receive, but "Occupy till I come" has special potential for good if rightly understood.

To many, "Occupy till I come" means "Sure, Jesus is coming soon, but let's not get too excited" or "Yes, I believe in the Second Coming, but that doesn't stop us from doing business as usual."

Now, it's true that the phrase does condemn a "Christ against culture" mind-set. It resists fanaticism and encourages a commonsense approach to living. But the primary meaning of the text is much more penetrating than that.

When Christ says "Occupy till I come," He is really declaring, "Here are funds that I want you to invest. I'm not telling you exactly how to use them, but I am expecting you to manage them wisely and to be able to show good returns when I ask for an accounting."

Or to put it another way: "These are important talents and opportunities that I am providing you, and someday I am going to judge you by the way that you have used them. Here is your life's investment—now, go out and obtain the maximum results."

That is the broad meaning of the parable of the pounds. But a detailed examination of the plot unearths a number of very special lessons. Notice first in verse 12 that the nobleman who went away represents Jesus, who was equal with God and was in the beginning with Him (John 1:1-3).

The country to which the nobleman was traveling symbolizes heaven, the throne room of the universe. Even as the nobleman journeyed to that country to receive a kingdom, that is, to be confirmed for rulership, so Christ has returned to heaven as conqueror.

His promise is: "I go to prepare a place for you. And if I go and prepare a place for you, I will come again, and receive you unto myself; that where I am, there ye may be also" (John 14:2, 3).

Also in verse 12 we see that the nobleman's destination is called a *far* country. A far country indicates a lengthy one—a warning of the many centuries that would evolve between Christ's departure and His return.

Observe also the analogies of verse 13. Note first that "he called his *ten* servants." Most Bible authorities agree that a nobleman of this stature would have had more servants than that, and that it is the symbolism of the number 10 that is important here.

Ten means completeness, and by 10 servants Christ represents the entire spectrum of church membership.

But verse 13 also states "he . . . delivered them ten pounds." A pound in Christ's time approximated a full day's wage, and thus represents the entire complement of gifts that the Holy Spirit distributes for fulfilling the master's assignments.

Verse 14 also has important symbols. It reads: "But his citizens hated him, and sent a message after him, saying, We will not have this man to reign over us."

Those who rejected the nobleman's authority represent the faithless of society—men and women who hear God's Word and consciously spurn His invitation to discipleship.

With this background in mind, we are now prepared to examine the dramatic climax of the drama—the day of appraisal and accountability when the nobleman returned and meted out judgment.

Verse 15 states: "And it came to pass, that when he returned, having received the kingdom, then he commanded these servants to be called unto him, to whom he had given the money, that he might know how much every man had gained by trading."

The nobleman's return depicts the hour of destiny when each of us will have our stewardship judged by God.

The first of the summoned servants appears in verse 16 and confidently reports, "Lord, thy pound hath gained ten pounds."

He then receives a rich reward.

To him the nobleman responds, "Well, thou good servant: because thou hast been faithful in a very little, have thou authority over ten cities."

Pleased with the servant's diligent obedience, the nobleman rewarded him richly.

The second servant reports in verse 18: "Lord, thy pound hath gained five pounds."

And in verse 19 the nobleman commends him: "Be thou also over five cities." His is not as rich a reward—in fact, the nobleman doesn't give him even a "Well done." But his judgment is positive.

That is not, however, the case with the third servant, who in verse 20 reports, "Lord, behold, here is thy pound, which I have kept laid up in a napkin."

He gives his excuses for failure in verse 21.

In verse 22 the disappointed ruler roundly condemns him, stripping him of his unused talent and classifying him with the wicked who had outright rejected him.

And what are the lessons for us today? First and foremost, we learn the nature of our discipleship. The servant who did not utilize his capital had a distorted view of himself, of his master, and of the relationship that existed between them.

His excuses in verse 21 were: "For I feared thee, because thou art an austere man: thou takest up that thou layest not down, and reapest that thou didst not sow."

The Living Bible puts it this way: "But the third man brought back only the money he had started with. 'I've kept it safe,' he said, 'because I was afraid [you would demand my profits], for you are a hard man to deal with, taking what isn't yours and even confiscating the crops that others plant'" (Luke 19:21).

The problem? He recoiled from absolute servanthood—the fact that the nobleman owned him totally—lock, stock, and barrel—and that all were to be returned to him.

The society in which he lived was not democratic, or capitalistic, or socialistic—as a citizen of a monarchy, he was a slave.

Then the owner was due not only the principal but also the interest on all investments. The money wasn't his—it was the nobleman's. He was to occupy or trade for his master's good—not his own.

We too are commissioned by a returning Lord. Equipped with talents and opportunities, we really don't possess—we occupy.

This house of time in which we live isn't really ours.

It all belongs to Christ—our minds, our energies, our personalities, our possessions, our knowledge, and our talents. God has entrusted us with all these gifts and more—they really belong to Him, and all the good that accrues from them must go to His glory.

The second lesson we can learn from the parable is the value of a positive view of the will of God. The servant's protest, "For I was constantly afraid of you because you are a stern . . . man; you pick up what you did not lay down, and you reap what you did not sow" (verse 21, Amplified) is a confession of cynicism and distrust.

His pessimism and lack of faith in the system nullified his enthusiasm, stifled his stewardship, and robbed him of rewards.

A dour view of God's purposes always depresses one's enthusiasm. One must believe that everything God does and desires is for our benefit if one is to be really productive in His service. With God or with anyone else, good relationships are built upon trust and confidence.

Unfortunately, however, we are more and more reflecting the attitudes whose distrust and dissatisfaction Matthew describes as exploding into violence against his fellow laborers (Matt. 24:48).

His attitude, as he awaited his master's return, was characterized not by earnest industry but by accusation, acrimony, and hostility.

We see such servants aptly described in Ellen White's statement: "Gossipers and news carriers are a terrible curse to . . . churches" (*Testimonies*, vol. 2, p. 466).

And again: "The spirit of gossip and talebearing is one of Satan's special agencies to sow discord and strife. . . . Brethren and sisters are too ready to talk of the faults and errors that they think exist in others. . . . The children of these complainers listen with open ears and receive the poison of disaffection" (*ibid.*, vol. 4, p. 195).

It's too bad that our campuses and communities are so often hotbeds of rumor and accusation. It's too bad our churches and institutions are so often deluged with unhappy tales of dissension and strife. Our irritability, our distrust, our turbulent disaffection, radically reduce the quality of our witness. Who would want to belong to a church with all the problems that we lay out before our children at Sabbath dinner?

All of us have contributed to the prevailing cynicism toward church leadership. But we are here today to learn, to grow, and to improve.

The lessons of the servants of the parable are pointed warnings against the ingratitude that decimates us. To be wounded or killed at the hand of the enemy is tragic indeed, but to be fired upon or bombed by "friendly" troops is even more pathetic. But that phenomenon increasingly marks our "last days" experience.

The third and final lesson of the parable is the folly of servile resignation.

The real tragedy of the unfaithful servant is that he did nothing—zero. He didn't even try. And that is the ultimate crime. The perfect crime is not breaking the law and leaving no clues behind. The perfect crime is going through life without wishing to grasp opportunity. In the final analysis, it is not really the volume of return that God rewards, but the effort.

Another way to put it is that God honors earnestness of endeavor not volume of results. "The approval of the Master is not given because of the greatness of the work performed, but because of fidelity in all that has been done" (*Gospel Workers*, p. 267).

In the secular realm one can earnestly try and utterly fail, but with God, to try earnestly is to succeed. Just avoiding evil is not enough. We are not saved by tying up our little talents and preserving them in a bundle, dodging opportunities so as to avoid mistakes.

"Occupy till I come" is a call to arms, a command to aggressive responsibility.

Occupiers do not spin their wheels and hedge their energies for fear of failure. Occupiers try—and that is what God rewards.

All occupiers will be rewarded at the Master's return.

Others may receive greater rewards, but even "less" in heaven is reward enough.

Far from being a hard taskmaster, the Nobleman is, in fact, a kindhearted Judge. He hears every prayer, sees every tear, rewards every good motive, and all who try—even with less visible results than others—are fulfilling His command—"Occupy till I come."

And we must not forget that the Nobleman who rewards His friends also recompenses His enemies. The God of manifold blessings is also the God of terrible vengeance.

While it is true that the "gift of God is eternal life," it is just as true that "the wages of sin is death." Failure to occupy or to trade on one's talents, is sin.

The basis of reward is not about the do's and don'ts of the meats and drinks of obedience. It is all about our investment portfolio—our use of our God-given stock. And while He is a loving God who faithfully honors what His servants have attempted, He is also an exacting God who repays all sloth—and punishes misuse of time and talent.

Because judgment against disobedience does not always come swiftly, an evil citizenry rejects God's rule, and faithless servants abuse their trust.

But judgment deferred is not judgment dismissed.

"He that shall come will come," and when the Nobleman returns, "there will be weeping and gnashing of teeth."

Those who betray the Master's trust and those who reject His rule will alike get recompensed with dreadful finality.

"Occupy till I come" is a solemn reminder of that fateful hour when we must all give account for our stewardship.

And what gives the Master such authority over our lives, such absolute right over our priorities? His dual ownership.

First, we are His by creation. As Creator/Owner, His are the inalienable rights of an absolute sovereign. His law is our guide, His character is our standard, His will is our mandate, His cause our obsession. His creative genius obligates us to service to Him as long as life shall last.

And we are His by redemption—transplanted from the kingdom of darkness to the kingdom of light—reconciled by His death and saved by His life (Rom. 5:10). The blood that flowed at Calvary is the coinage that bought us back. Once captives of darkness, now citizens of light, we are fanatically constrained to fulfill His command: "Occupy till I come!"

Chapter 5

FROM RAGS TO RICHES

"And he carried me away in the spirit to a great and high mountain, and shewed me that great city, the holy Jerusalem, descending out of heaven from God, having the glory of God: and her light was like unto a stone most precious, even like a jasper stone, clear as crystal; and had a wall great and high, and had twelve gates, and at the gates twelve angels, and names written thereon, which are the names of the twelve tribes of the children of Israel" (Rev. 21:10-12).

Scripture depicts the plan of salvation in many ways—none more poignantly than the saga of the 12 tribes of Israel.

In both their number "12" (which in Bible symbolism indicates "chosen totality") and in their histories, the tribes speak eloquently to the triumphs and tragedies of the saved.

Jacob's dying charge to his sons (Gen. 49) and Moses' later farewell to their posterity (Deut. 33) provide an accurate portrayal not only of their pilgrimage, but valuable lessons for our own.

Jacob describes his first son, Reuben, as kind, magnanimous, and peace-loving. Reuben's attempt to rescue Joseph from the brothers' murderous conspiracy at Dothan demonstrates these characteristics. However, his principal weakness, instability, to a large degree neutralized his good traits.

Thus, Jacob prophesied of him: "Reuben, thou art my firstborn, my might, . . . unstable as water, thou shalt not excel" (Gen. 49:3, 4).

Simeon and Levi are jointly portrayed. Their strength, described by Jacob as their patriotism, had memorable demonstration in the Levites' stand against idolatry at the incident of the golden calf and in Simeon's role in the drama on Mount Gerizim (Deut. 27:12).

Their weakness, extreme cruelty, also noted by Jacob, was reflected in Simeon's prominent role in the enslavement of Joseph and in the brothers' heartless slaughter of the Shechemites (Gen. 34:25).

Judah is extolled by his father as decisive and dependable. But his weakness, immorality, revealed itself in his adulterous conduct with Tamar, his daughter-in-law (Gen. 38:18), and in the promiscuity of his subsequent descendants, including the moral tragedies of King David, a product of this tribe.

The strength of Zebulun was valor. This is the tribe that fought so heroically with Barak against Sisera (Judges 4), with Gideon against the Midianites (Judges 6), and with David against his enemies (1 Chron. 12). Their weakness, wanderlust or an itinerant nature, Moses spoke of as their "going out" (Deut. 33:18).

Jacob commended Issachar and his descendants as faithful burdenbearers (Gen. 49:14). However, as history shows, their lack of initiative reduced them to servants of tribute (verse 15).

Jacob said of Dan: He "shall judge his people" (verse 16). And it was so. They were the intellectual aristocracy of Israel. But their weaknesses, criticism and idolatry, were also pronounced.

Jacob's words concerning Gad were that "a troop shall overcome him: but he shall overcome at the last" (verse 19). The success of the Gadites in surviving in the distinctly disadvantaged terrain that they chose on the east side of Jordan confirms the prophecy of their unique ability to persevere. Gad's weakness, bad judgment, is seen in his tribe's unwise choice of settling on the eastern shores of Jordan, a territory which isolated them from the rest of God's people.

Moses spoke of Asher, whose name means "happy" or "good" disposition, as being particularly blessed. "Let Asher be blessed with children; let him be acceptable to his brethren." Asher's weakness, noted by Deborah, was noninvolvement. When characterizing this people's relationship to duty and crises, she said: "Asher sat still on the sea coast, and remained by his creeks. [These came not forth to battle for God's people]" (Judges 5:17, Amplified Version).

In addressing Napthali, Jacob said he would be a people of "goodly words" (Gen. 49:21), and Moses said that they should be a people "satisfied with favor" and "full with the blessing of the Lord" (Deut. 33:23). Neither Jacob nor Moses mention the weakness of this son and his posterity, but subsequent history reveals them as a people of ingratitude. They failed to appreciate God's favor and shared generously in Christ's scathing rebuke of the ungrateful and unrepentant (Matt. 11:22-24).

Praised by Jacob as a fruitful bough (Gen. 49:22) and by Moses as a recipient of precious gifts (Deut. 33:13-17), Joseph demonstrated sterling qualities of diligence, honesty, and administrative ability. The strongest suggestion of weakness in his personality is his apparent emotional softness. We are not surprised that at age 37, after

20 years of separation, nostalgia overwhelmed him when he was reunited with his family. That it was more than the usual is suggested by the fact that he not only wept when he first saw his brothers (Gen. 42:24), but when they prepared to return home to Jacob (verse 24), when they returned with Benjamin (Gen. 43:30), when he revealed himself to them (Gen. 45:2), when he embraced Benjamin (verse 14), when he again greeted his brothers (verse 15), when he met his father (Gen. 46:29), at the death of his father (Gen. 50:1), and when after his father's death his brothers expressed fear of him (verse 17).

Benjamin, described by Moses as "beloved of the Lord" (Deut. 33:12), was a tribe gifted with high artistic and athletic ability (Judges 20:15, 16; 1 Chron. 12:2). Its weakness, alluded to in Moses' characterization of them as being "raven as wolves," was stealth, impetuosity, and stubbornness. The latter they demonstrated in Judges 20, when they refused to deliver for punishment the Gibeathites, who had abused the Levite's concubine and then with predictably disastrous consequences went to war against the other 11 tribes.

And what are the summary lessons of this colorful history for you and me today?

First of all, Scripture reminds us that sin's consequences are more the logical results of its character than the arbitrary vengeance of God. We see this demonstrated in the experience of each of the tribes. Unstable Reuben furnished no judge, no prophet, and, with the exception of Adina and the 30 men ranked among the valiant in David's army (1 Chron. 11:42), no national heroes.

Vindictive Simeon fathered a tribe that suffered great violence throughout their history. God's promise "I will divide them . . . and scatter them in Israel" (Gen. 49:7) poignantly met its fulfillment. Torn by internal dissension, the tribe finally disintegrated under the weight of its heated animosities (Num. 25) and was, for all practical purposes, absorbed by Judah (1 Chron. 4:27, 39, 42).

The Levites were also scattered and given no inheritance in Canaan. Their fate would, no doubt, have been as depressing as that of Simeon but for the fact that a strong conscience regarding holy things tempered their cruelty. The incident of the golden calf earned for them the priesthood (Ex. 32:26-29), but their territorial disenfranchisement perpetually reminded them of the sure effects of a vengeful spirit.

Sensual Judah, mentioned in the Old Testament more than any other tribe except Joseph, prevailed above the other tribes (1 Chron. 5:2). However, the lust of the flesh, which stained the careers of David, Solomon, and others of his lineage, brought bitter recriminations to his posterity.

Wandering Zebulun's toleration of evil (Judges 1:30) led to a destructive accommodation to heathenism. And while they were valiant in battle, they became widely known for their worldliness.

Issachar's descendants, a people who knew "what Israel ought to do" (1 Chron. 12:32), settled as one of the smallest and poorest of the tribes, though often ranked ahead of Zebulun, his older and full-blooded brother (Deut. 33:18, 19). Zebulun's indifference denied him and his descendants any significant contribution to Israel's history.

Judgmental Dan, who left his children a legacy of censoriousness, produced—as might be expected—a people of harsh and critical attitude. As is often the case with those most critical of others, they were, in fact, themselves guilty of sins greater than those they attacked. Dan was the first of the tribes to introduce idolatry among God's people (Judges 18:30).

Unwise Gad, who with Reuben and Manasseh settled on the east side of the Jordan, paid for their faulty judgment with centuries of physical and material hardship.

Materialistic Asher fathered a tribe whose preoccupation for gain doomed them to spiritual poverty.

Ungrateful Napthali's insensitivity to God's leading eventuated in compromise with lesser cultures and a peripheral part in the life of Israel.

Joseph's extreme emotionalism appears to have muted his capacity for an outstanding posterity. As is often the case with strong leaders, none of his children approximated his stellar career.

The pugnacity and stubbornness of Benjamin meant that they were almost decimated by warfare. Through most of biblical history it remained not only the smallest but in many ways the most insignificant of the tribes.

Clearly, we do reap what we sow. What we call the blessings and curses of God are more often than not the natural predictable consequences of our own choices, our own actions—not the capricious acts of God or what some see as happenstance or "circumstance." A second lesson to be learned from Israel's tribal history is the interdependence of spiritual fellowship.

We glean this from their placement around the tabernacles (Num. 2). This arrangement gave needed balanced to the varied personalities we have noted.

On the east Judah's firm administrative personality reenforced the docile character of Issachar and the itinerant nature of Zebulun. On the other hand, Zebulun's valor encouraged Issachar, and Issachar's fidelity was instructive for Zebulun's wanderlust and Judah's lustful philandering.

To the south the pacifying ways of thoughtful Reuben mitigated the cruel tendencies of Simeon and the extreme independence of Gad. On the other hand,

Simeon's patriotism countered Reuben's indecisiveness and Gad's pugnacity while Gad's perseverance encouraged both of his more impulsive brothers.

On the north studious Dan stimulated serious thought among the materialistic descendants of Asher and the blessed but unthankful children of Napthali. Happy Asher counterbalanced the negativism of both Dan and Napthali. Napthali's ability to communicate no doubt often enhanced the narrow-minded Dan and materialistic Asher.

On the west were Ephraim and Manasseh who fulfilled God's promise to their father Joseph of a "double portion." In this association the aggressive Ephraim who grew to be second only to Judah in power stimulated his more passive brother, Manasseh, and was a corrective agent to the stubborn isolationist, Benjamin. On the other hand, the retiring and humble Manasseh softened the haughtiness of Ephraim and Benjamin and the latter both benefited from Benjamin's spontaneity and creativity.

It should be clear: we are our brothers' keepers. The impersonalization of modern times must not obscure the obligation of mutual support within the ranks of God's people. It is as dangerous for us moderns to "confess our faults one to another" as it is to greet each other with "a holy kiss." Nevertheless, we cannot grow or even survive without each other. "We sustain a loss when we neglect the privilege of associating together to strengthen and encourage one another in the service of God . . . He who shuts himself up to himself is not filling the position that God designed he should. The proper cultivation of the social elements in our nature brings us into sympathy with others and as a means of development and strength to us in the service of God" (*Steps to Christ*, p. 101).

Third, we learn the lesson of God's power to forgive and restore. So proud is Christ of these prototypical representatives of our race that He engraves each of their names above one of the 12 gates of the Holy City (Rev. 21:12). They are there not just for their reward but for our encouragement as well. And many believe each of us will enter the glory kingdom through the gate bearing the name of the tribe whose characteristics we most closely resemble.

John lists the tribes' names on Heaven's gates in joyous celebration of God's saving grace (Rev. 7:5-8). On the gates are listed unstable Reuben (verse 5); cruel Simeon and Levi (verse 7); sensual Judah (verse 5); ungrateful Napthali (verse 6); the warlike Gadites (verse 5); the materialistic Asherites (verse 6); the docile Issacharites (verse 7); the wandering Zebulunites (verse 8); the softhearted Josephites (verse 8); the stubborn Benjaminites (verse 8); and the colorless, bypassed people of Manasseh (verse 6).

It is revealing to note that of the original 12, the book of Revelation omits only Dan, the talented but mean-spirited critic. It is of further interest that Ephraim, who shared Dan's other sinful trait of idolatry, is also missing.

They made it! Every single tribe named except the two noted and the specially assigned Levites is there. Though afflicted with what our prophet calls "inbred sin," and though often, especially in their youth, demonstrating weaknesses that brought reverses and disappointment, each repented and was forgiven. Each, in spite of the tendencies of evil he had been born with, became an overcomer and was accepted, washed by the blood, and covered by the robe of Jesus.

So it is not to the enormity of our faults that we must look—it is to the greatness of God's forgiveness, to the fact that the church is indeed a "theater of God's grace."

Let us rejoice that the church is not a "deep freeze for the saints," but a "hospital for sinners," and that through Christ we are saved from the "guttermost to the uttermost"—from the "ridiculous to the sublime"—from "rags to riches."

Chapter 6

THE PARADOXES OF SUCCESS

"And he that taketh not his cross, and followeth after me is not worthy of me. He that findeth his life shall lose it: and he that loseth his life for my sake shall find it" (Matt. 10:38, 39).

A paradox is "an argument that derives conflicting conclusions by valid deductions from acceptable premises"—or to put it more simply, a paradox is a statement of truth presented in contradictory language. Christ, the greatest teacher of them all, often used this method.

Such is the case with our text when Jesus said, "He that findeth his life shall lose it: and he that loseth his life for my sake shall find it." Or again when He said, "If any man desire to be first, the same shall be last" (Mark 9:35).

Christ's statements of paradox are not so numerous or often remembered as His parables—the good Samaritan, the ten virgins, the prodigal son, etc. But they are no less helpful to our understandings of truth.

While today's culture is vastly different from that of Christ's time, the use of paradoxes in spiritual learning is as instructive now as it was then. In fact, there are three commonsense paradoxes that I wish to present today that we find particularly geared to our times.

The first is: *We must go down in order to go up.*

A very unfortunate aspect of our age is what some call the "instant syndrome." We have not only instant coffee, instant communications, instant relief (if we would believe the TV ads), but also instant food, instant riches, instant knowledge, instant love, instant marriage, and consequently, instant divorce. And the instant syndrome seems to have taken hold of our work ethic as well. Superficiality, or second-rate productivity characterizes our mentality so thoroughly that appearance has become more valued than substance, titles more important than techniques, position more honored than process, and power more sought than principle.

The Paradoxes of Success

Nowadays it doesn't matter what's inside the package as long as the wrapper looks good. But I wish to remind us that real excellence and results that endure require energy, effort, and, often, a good deal of sacrifice.

My church history teacher in college was fond of saying, "Time doth not honor that which is done without her participation." And oh, how true! There is no such thing in life as instant quality.

Michelangelo once said, "If people only knew how hard I worked to get my mastery, it wouldn't seem so wonderful after all."

Vince Lombardi is quoted as having said that the difference between success and failure is not talent but the willingness to sacrifice and to work hard in developing one's abilities. And on the golf course we have an expression that says, "The more I practice, the luckier I get."

If we would really achieve, we must remember that "attitude determines altitude," that the deeper and broader the foundations, the higher the building can rise. Shallow foundations make for shallow careers.

To make a meaningful contribution requires meaningful effort. To be the best that one can be demands deferred gratification—that is, making present sacrifices in order to attain future rewards.

In order to go up, one must go down—down deep into the well of education. You must drill faithfully into the gold mines of literature and history and science and never forget that the strength and height of life's edifice is directly proportional to the breadth and depth of its foundation. "You must go down in order to go up."

The second paradox that I wish to offer states: *We must give in order to gain.*

Another destructive force in society today is what is known as the acquisitive mentality. The acquisitive spirit says, "Get all you can, and can all you get." Such selfishness destroys scruples and leads to the belief that "anything goes."

That spirit not only shifts the energies once directed for spiritual ends into material goals, it substitutes its own system of rewards, so that we regard the rich as blessed and the poor as condemned by God.

Contemporary society no longer seeks to develop the inner spiritual forces that make for justice, fraternity, public peace, and individual happiness. Rather, its chief goal is the glitter and the tinsel of surface trappings. Its modus operandi is "If it sounds good, try it"; "If it looks good, buy it"; "If it feels good, do it"—"Eat, drink, and be merry, for tomorrow you may die."

Ours is a "thingified" society—one in which conspicuous consumption, conspicuous leisure, and conspicuous waste has become the badge of success; one in which traditional values such as family relations have crumpled under the weight of our materialistic preoccupations.

As a consequence of our frantic efforts to keep up with the Joneses and stay ahead of the Smiths, the home is no longer an "end" in which family members satisfy common needs. It is rather a "means"—a way-station—from which we leave to engage in those activities elsewhere. We have parceled education to schools, our religions to churches, our recreation to sporting arenas, and our eating to fast-food restaurants. And what little time for togetherness our schedules allow at home we spend locked, zombie-like, onto the sordid offerings of TV.

The quest for materialism is difficult to resist, but there are shining examples of those who do refuse to succumb.

One such person is the physician whom my wife and I met several years ago on a visit to West Africa. There at Massanga, our leper colony in the Sierra Leone, we encountered a young, highly skilled physician and musician who, with his wife and two sons, is giving himself in sacrificial ministry to lepers.

Now, I don't know if you have seen leprosy. I had not until then. It is a gruesome and dreadful disease. It destroys the nerve endings in the hands and feet so that the victim continuously injures him or her self without realizing it. The cutting, burning, bruising, and abusing of the extremities until finally it causes them to decay and rot away with a sickening stench.

But here in this forest region of a foreign land—literally spending his life on a mission of mercy—is this remarkably unselfish man and his family.

I had the privilege of walking the wards of the leprosarium with him. As he made his rounds, I saw him press the sores and open the abscesses. While I watched he tenderly cared for these helpless humans, exposing himself to the infection that breeds in such places.

Even now I marvel at his surrender of himself and his family to the hardships and uncertainties of life in that colony of death. His professional skills are capable of providing him with lavish comforts back home in Sweden. But instead he has refused riches and acclaim and has given his life in service to others.

That is the way God intended it. Consider the cycles of nature by which He models the principle of sharing.

First the sun soaks up the moisture from the ocean and it condenses into clouds. Then, pregnant with their misty burden, heavy clouds burst with thunderclaps and shower upon the mountains and hills. The water this produces cascades in falls and brooks and streams down the hillsides, enriching farms and fields along the way before finally settling into the ocean below. Then the sun once more absorbs the moisture that condenses into clouds, and the process repeats itself over and over again.

And that cycle is typical of the way that God has made everything on Earth to contribute to the good of others. It is the basic law of human happiness as well. Yes, "it *is* more blessed to give than to receive."

The standard for all existence is that "God so loved that He gave," and we must never forget that at life's end what really matters is not the extent of our bank account or how much acreage we own or how many positions we've held. We will then be judged not by how many goods we have amassed but how much good we have shared, given our opportunities for service.

So I challenge you as you plan for the future. Do so with some worthwhile cause in mind—some mission bigger than yourself. Decide that what you are going to do will have as its primary objective not your aggrandizement but the betterment of humanity. Remember, what makes the Dead Sea stagnant is its lack of outlet. The waters collect with nowhere to go. It receives but does not give.

It is paradoxical but true that the more you give, the more you gain. The more of yourself that you employ for the good of others, the more your talents will grow, and the greater will be your personal rewards. "You must give in order to gain!"

The third and final paradox states: *"We must surrender in order to be free."*

We often hear the cry for freedom in our age. Youth want to be free, minorities want to be free, women want to be free, labor wants to be free, the handicapped want to be free—and of course, they all should be. Christians should participate in such struggles for relief from unjust social and psychological constraints.

But may I remind you of the parallel truth that in matters of faith, to be free is to be bound, not by arbitrary rules, but by the just principles of God's law.

There are, of course, several classifications of law: civil law, natural law, and, of course, moral law. But think about it. One isn't free when breaking any of these laws. As demonstrated with civil law, it's when you get ticketed for its violation that you are no longer free.

The same applies to the natural world. We are not free when we abuse our bodies—eating the wrong things and otherwise dissipating and mistreating them. We are free only when we rest well and eat well and care for ourselves properly. Only then do we escape the penalties and the sufferings of our transgressions. The same is true with the laws of God, the laws of Holy Scripture.

Many youth approach the question of law and freedom like the young man brought up in a strict Christian home who lamented when he came of age and said:

Go On!

"My mother told me not to smoke; I don't.
Or listen to a naughty joke; I don't.
She told me that I must not think
About intoxicating drink;
At pretty girls I must not wink; I don't.

Wild youth chase women, wine, and song; I don't.
To stay up late is very wrong, I don't.
I kiss no girls, not even one.
I do not know how it is done;
You wouldn't think I have much fun—I don't!"

He had it all wrong—God's laws do not put us in the straitjacket of joylessness. Rather, they deliver us from the pitfalls of evil. They tell us: "Slow down, danger ahead! Yield, trouble is coming." They steer us around the harrowing curves in the mountains of life. They protect us when entering the dark tunnels of trial. They warn us when we are speeding toward the dead end of transgression. And if we can learn to benefit from the past, if we would be wise enough to look at the accumulated wisdom of the ages and live by those laws, we will be happier and more productive persons.

It is the perversion of freedom—not its quest—that is confusing society today. When people kick off the traces—when individuals come to believe that there are no final judgments, no absolutes, no sacred standards, that conventionality is unfairly restrictive—it is license for which they grasp, not freedom.

We cannot call it freedom when the laws of the land are so structured that criminal conviction is nearly impossible—even when caught in the act. Nor is it freedom when Nazis demonstrate on our streets under police protection. Freedom does not permit sordid, selfish, sick, insensitive minds to design pornography and disseminate it throughout our communities, inundating our society with filth. That is license—not true freedom.

So you want to be free? Well, fine, but remember that the only way to be truly free—free from unnecessary illness, free from guilt, free from disillusionment, free from the debilitating effects that inevitably follow the breach of the moral laws of the universe, free from the anger of the all-powerful God who has given you that beautiful life and provided you the rules for its care—is to respect His law and live up to its requirements. Yes, "You must surrender in order to be free."

We have noted that Jesus taught by paradox as well as parable. But more grandly to the human mind, Christ's ministry, itself, is a cosmic paradox. His ministry for us is truth stated in language that is contradictory to our reason: King of the universe and homeless Servant; Maker of oceans and the thirsty Suppliant; Commander of legions and humble Captive; Maker of the law and Ransom for sin; Offering Priest and offered sacrifices; Lion of Judah and Lamb of God; Creator and Redeemer; all Divine and all Human; Ancient of Days dying in His youth; Light of the universe engulfed by the darkness of Calvary.

Such love defies human logic. We do not now—nor shall we ever—fully comprehend how it could be, but with faith's eye, we see in His person the miracle of opposites that produces our salvation. In Him we witness the polarities that fuse into redemption.

It is left now for us to cling to His promise and to follow in His footsteps, always seeing "through a glass, darkly," but relentlessly pursuing the wisdom that teaches we must go down to go up, that we give to gain, and that we surrender to be free!

Chapter 7

HABITS

"Can a black man change the color of his skin, or a leopard remove its spots. If they could, then you that do nothing but evil could learn to do what is right" (Jer. 13:23, *NEB*).

I would like to discuss with you a word that experience shows has more to do with success in this world and entrance into the next than most of us realize. It's not an easy word to deal with, because we all stand condemned and embarrassed beneath the glare of its hard, inflexible rays. And yet it is a word that we need to openly confront and candidly engage from time to time. This little, powerful, pungent, potent word is "habit"!

What is habit? It is one's usual behavior or course of action, an act so frequently repeated that it becomes an acquired tendency. A habit is a practice that by repetition becomes customary—what the psychologists call a reflex or involuntary response.

Of course, all of us are all creatures of habit, and it is a good thing that we are. Life would be impossibly complex if we had to pause and think about each succeeding action. Nature has equipped us with marvelous reflex mechanisms. This system of nerve memory allows us to live today's agenda guided by the stored patterns of yesterday's experiences.

Every time we repeat an action, we reinforce it. So then, what we do, from the sound of the alarm clock in the morning till we fall asleep at night, is mainly a series of subconscious responses—doing things again and again the way we've done them a thousand times before.

Many—especially the young—try to defy the dictates of habit. They view what they have done and what they will do as independent, unrelated phenomena. For them, life is a series of isolated decisions—individual choices made as circumstances may attract or demand. But it is not so! As our text reminds us, we are guided by directives as hard to undo as the Black man changing his skin or the leopard his spots.

Thus, Thomas Carlyle could say, "Habit is the deepest law of nature." Horace Mann said, "Habit is a cable. We weave a thread of it every day, and at last we cannot break it." Samuel Johnson said, "The chains of habit are generally too small to be felt until they are too strong to be broken." E. F. Benson declared, "We all think we can choose when the choice comes, but our choice is really made not at the moment, but . . . you choose according to that which you have chosen a hundred times before." And Ellen White cooborates: "The character is formed, to a great extent, in early years. The habits then established have more influence than any natural endowment" (*Child Guidance*, p. 199).

Of the many clusters or classifications of habit that it is possible to identify, nothing is more vital to our well-being than our habits of health.

Poor habits are the reason for most of life's spiritual and physical misery. Good health is not, as so many seem to think, simply a matter of genetics or chance. True, we are not all equal in strength. Some are blessed with more vital force than others. Further, even healthy bodies are vulnerable to the diseases and accidents that are not one's fault. Health habits involve, therefore, not so much to one's longevity as to the quality of care one exercises with the measure of strength God has given. And how do we achieve that? By proper diet, balanced exercise, sufficient rest, etc.

Ignoring such principles brings accurate fulfillment of the wise man's warning: "As the bird by wandering, as the swallow by flying, so the curse causeless shall not come" (Prov. 26:2).

Another category of habit contributing more to earthly success and heavenly reward than we commonly realize surfaces in the following quotations: "It is the work of parents to train their children to proper habits of speech" (*Christ's Object Lessons*, p. 337).

"The power of speech is a talent that should be diligently cultivated. Of all the gifts we have received from God, none is capable of being a greater blessing than this. . . . By diligent effort all may acquire the power to read intelligently, and to speak in a full, clear, round tone, in a distinct and impressive manner" (*ibid.*, pp. 335, 336).

The late Eva B. Dykes, Ph.D., a perfectionist in this regard, taught us a little jingle back in freshman composition that described a particularly attractive but inarticulate female as follows: "But when she spoke, the charm was broke."

Black English has its place. In some circumstances, colloquial expressions may actually be more effective than standard English or even the Queen's English, if you please. But while Black pride allows us to preserve what is unique and valuable in our heritage, it should not cause us to disdain time-honored standards of grammatical excellence. There is such a thing as proper speech, a preferred style of communication—and every one of us should strive for proficiency in it.

Of course, it is not easy for some. Years of improper speech patterns plow almost ineradicable grooves along the surface of the cortex, where speech activity originates. It takes Herculean effort to rechannel these impulses into new tracks. But we must try, and the best ways to do so are (1) listening to speakers who articulate properly, and (2) daily practice, as in audible reading—particularly of the Bible. Believe it or not— 10 minutes a day of audible Bible reading will do more to correct one's speech habits than Speech 101, and will, not too incidentally, groove in some life-sustaining principles in the process.

The third category of habits recommends itself in the following advice:

"All who will may overcome these fussy, lingering habits. In their work let them have a definite aim. Decide how long a time is required for a given task, and then bend every effort toward accomplishing the work in the given time. The exercise of the will power will make the hands move deftly" (*ibid.*, p. 344).

It is true that work fascinates some people. They can sit and watch it for hours! Others, because of habits of haste, superficiality, and dishonesty, prostitute their time and talents for meager gain. Such individuals make a mockery of the fact that God gave us work as a means of developing our physical, mental, and spiritual powers. Truly there are few satisfactions comparable to that of a job well done. Solomon had that in mind when he said, "The sleep of a laboring man is sweet."

Finally, may I recommend a habit that will enhance not only those we have already considered but all other habits as well. The following quotation explains it:

"Our God is a God of order, and He desires that His children shall *will* to bring themselves into order and under His discipline. . . . If the youth would form habits of regularity and order, they would improve in health, in spirits, in memory, and in disposition" (*Child Guidance*, p. 112).

What do we mean by regularity and order? It involves "planning your work and working your plans." Developing right priorities, we take a structured approach to our use of time. We will not stumble through the day striking out here and there at activities that may attract us, much like someone moving along the aisles of a supermarket and impulsively throwing items into the basket.

We must not respond helter-skelter to the clutter of challenges that beckon us each day. We must make conscious decisions as to how to utilize our resources of time and energy. We must refuse to let pretty but petty activities sidetrack us from life's primary quests.

Some people fail to budget their finances, and they don't know "where the month went at the end of the money." Others squander their time and cannot account for their efforts at the end of the day, the end of the year, and, sadly, at the end of their lives.

Habits

The regularity of the universe, the unalterable rhythm of the seasons, the predictability of the galaxies, the reliability of the laws that sustain the cosmos—all tell us that we serve a God of detail and order, a God of unerring dependability and order. But it is not just in His divine activities that we witness such regularity. It was in His human existence as well.

We see in the life of our Lord an economy and precision of words, as manifested in the Sermon on the Mount; a concern for ecology and conservation of resources, as witnessed in the gathering of the fragments after He fed the multitudes; and a predisposition to tidiness and detail, as demonstrated by the grave clothes neatly folded in His tomb.

But His human life was more than a life of orderly care—it was a ministry timely fulfilled.

Jesus met with exact precision every prophecy of His birth, His life, His service, His death, His resurrection, and His return to the Father. The order that He exhibited in His earthly life and the regularity with which He guides His physical universe constantly rebuke and challenge our habits of sloth and selfishness.

But what makes habits of order so vital is the fact that they are not simply a vehicle for personal advancement. Rather, they provide structure and essence to our spiritual restoration. "Actions repeated form habits, habits form character, and by the character our destiny for time and for eternity is decided" (*Christ's Object Lessons*, p. 356).

We are all sinful beings with diseased egos. Afflicted with inherited weaknesses, we are by nature disposed to sin and transgression. Then, further polluted by the weight of cultivated evil, we deepen our predisposition to disobedience until we find ourselves bound in wickedness as with cords of iron. And the longer we live in sin, the stronger the cords and the more difficult it is to change. And yet change we must. Somewhere between the cradle and the grave there must be what Paul called a "renewing of our mind"—a reversal of the process of self-annihilation.

It is this seemingly impossible effort that Jeremiah's question addresses. No, a Black man cannot change his skin. He may bleach his skin, but it is not permanent—as many a disillusioned Black found out in earlier times when "White was right" and Black was not beautiful.

However, Jeremiah's analogy is not absolute. There is hope. Listen to the voice of wisdom:

"Jesus will be the helper of all who put their trust in Him. . . . Bad habits, when opposed, will offer the most vigorous resistance; but if the warfare is kept up with energy and perseverance, they may be conquered" (*Testimonies*, vol. 4, p. 655).

And what is the secret of change—the "sufficient cause" of morality, as Aristotle would term it? It is the principle detailed by Paul, who wrote: "But we all, with open face beholding as in a glass the glory of the Lord, are changed into the same image from glory to glory even as by the Spirit of the Lord" (2 Cor. 3:18).

Jeremiah beheld our bondage and lamented, "Is there no balm in Gilead?" Is there no physician to cure our disease? But the redeemed of all ages attest in glad testimonial—"Yes, by beholding we become changed." And what is the secret of beholding? It is being constant in prayer and study of God's Word. In other words, establishing good habits of devotion—setting aside a regular (preferably each morning) time for personal Bible study and prayer (preferably at the same place) each day.

But it is more than the regularity implied in personal family and public worship. It is engaging in incessant, unceasing communion throughout the day. Jesus who went into the Temple "as His custom was" often spent whole nights in conversation with God, and if Jesus had to pray, what about us?

And what is the result of habitual communion? Again, to quote the prophet, "to the secret place of the most high, under the shadow of the almighty, men now and then repair; they abide for a season, and the result is manifest in noble deed; then their faith fails, the communion is interrupted, and the life work is marred. But the life of Jesus was a life of constant trust, sustained by continual communion; and His service for heaven and earth was without failure or faltering" (*Messages to Young People*, p. 117). That is the witness of restored extortioners such as Jacob and Simon, of reclaimed harlots such as Rahab and Mary, and of murderers such as Moses and David.

James and John, the vengeful sons of thunder, can vouch for it. Mercenary Matthew, the zealot Simeon, impulsive Peter, timid Philip, suspicious Thomas, and all the other disciples testify to God's recreative power.

Yes, there is a way out of the clutches of our inherited and cultivated evil. We can have escape from the iron bands of disastrous habits. That deliverance is available through Jesus, who alone has power to fill in the old grooves of sin and establish new channels where healthy habits flow.

"Can the Ethiopian change his skin, or the leopard his spots?" Can we, "accustomed to do evil," learn to do good?

No—that is, not of ourselves—but in Christ victory is possible. He is the antidote for all our diseases, the cure for our ills, the balm for all our afflictions. A sure solution, a proven prescription, an unfailing guide, He is a promise we must believe, an offer we cannot refuse—our only hope for the change that maximizes earthly opportunities and guarantees everlasting life.

Chapter 8

"WHATSOEVER A MAN SOWETH, THAT SHALL HE ALSO REAP"

"Be not deceived; God is not mocked: for whatsoever a man soweth, that shall he also reap" (Gal. 6:7).

W e usually associate this scripture with revenge and retribution. By it we remind ourselves and warn others that "God doesn't like ugly," and that He is certain to repay evil with evil, and that wrong deeds will inevitably boomerang upon the head of the perpetrator. For many this text boils down to: "That's all right, you did me wrong, but God knows, and you'll get yours some day one way or the other."

Perhaps this is a legitimate use of this verse in some circumstances. But it is surely not its only or even its primary intent. In fact, we severely cheapen Galatians 6:7 when we relegate it to a God-will-even-the-score-with-you kind of application.

What the apostle is really saying here is not "You kick my cat, and God will kill your dog," but rather "Look, I've studied this thing. I've read and watched, and I've come to the conclusion that life is enduringly a matter of cause and effect—that the same inflexible, immutable laws that govern the physical universe also rule in the moral realm. As planting determines the harvest in the natural world, so the spiritual crops of the moral universe are the sure results of our individual doings—'Whatsoever a man soweth that shall he also reap.'"

Notice first the nature of the sowing—*"Whatsoever* a man soweth." Every possible variety of seed will produce its harvest. The physical, intellectual, and spiritual seeds that we daily sow determine tomorrow's reaping. It is not only the way of nature, but of all of life.

But "whatsoever" has also to do with size. To this end Paul is saying, "No matter how small or seemingly insignificant the seed you scatter, it too will bring results."

We humans tend to watch for the larger challenges, the bolder temptations and battles, and ignore the common, seemingly insignificant encounters with duty. But it is a fact that "every word you utter, every act you perform, is a seed which will bear good or evil fruit, and will result in joy or sorrow to the sower" (*Messages to Young People*, p. 146); and that "The little foxes . . . spoil the vines" (S. of Sol. 2:15).

There is life in every germ of thought and every kernel of decision. In the moral universe smaller seeds will sprout no less certainly than the larger ones—"Whatsoever a man soweth, that shall he also reap."

Another major emphasis suggests itself in Paul's use of the demonstrative adjective "that." Here the accent shifts from the nature of the sowing, "*Whatsoever* a man soweth," to the character of the harvest itself. "Whatsoever a man soweth, *that* shall he also reap"!

The seed predetermines the quality of the harvest. Moral seed is either flesh or spirit, and they are mutually exclusive. All of our sowing is of one kind or the other. In fact, Paul continues, "For he that soweth to his flesh shall of the flesh reap corruption; but he that soweth to the Spirit shall of the Spirit reap life everlasting" (Gal. 6:8).

"Flesh sowing" is following the whims of the natural man—yielding to the temptations of the carnal nature. It is responding to the urges of selfishness and of passion and pride.

"Flesh reaping" is a distorted mind, clouded reasoning, a guilty conscience, and a bad reputation. Sowing to the flesh is intemperance at night; reaping is fighting to stay awake in class the next day. Sowing to the flesh is dancing in the dark; reaping is the headache and hangover when the lights come back on. Sowing to the flesh is a too-warm embrace; reaping is venereal disease and an uncontrollable desire for sexual variety. Sowing to the flesh is ingesting drugs, eating forbidden foods, and/or drinking alcoholic beverages; reaping is reduced reason, self-control, and lessened longevity.

Sowing to the Spirit is, of course, the antithesis of all this. It is living joyfully and abundantly by God's rules. It is not asceticism and abandonment of the real life, but rather placing godly values at the top of our list of priorities and being guided by them. Sowing to the Spirit is having worship every morning; reaping is daily growth in spiritual muscle and overcoming temptation. Sowing to the Spirit is eating correctly—on time, with proper quality and quantity; reaping is a healthy body, a clear mind, and undimmed spiritual vision. Sowing to the Spirit is going to bed on time; reaping is waking up with a clear head and mind. Sowing to the Spirit is attending class faithfully and taking homework seriously; reaping is receiving good grades, and enjoying knowledge and sharpened life skills.

"Whatsoever a Man Soweth, That Shall He Also Reap"

Those who live by the flesh flow downstream with the crowd—in the broad way of convenience and pleasure. But those who live by the Spirit fight against the current, choosing rather to travel in the narrow way of obedience and courage.

Nature is a bank that pays off with dividends. Our deeds accrue interest from the date of deposit—the moment we act—for the rest of our lives, and not just in kind but in greatly increased volume.

"In the harvest the seed is multiplied. A single grain of wheat, increased by repeated sowings, would cover a whole land with golden sheaves. So widespread may be the influence of a single life, of even a single act" (*Education*, p. 109).

What did you sow, Lot? The selfish act of choosing what seemed the richest terrain and pitching your tent "toward Sodom." And how did you reap? The loss of your family to the worldly society of the cities of the plain.

What did you sow, Jacob? Shrewdness in business, including the theft of your brother's birthright and blessings. And how did you reap? Disappointment in marriage, confiscation of your herds, dread of your brother, denial of seeing your mother again, and the scheming of your sons in Joseph's enslavement.

And what is it that you have sown, ye dusty sons of Ham? ye Canaanites? ye Egyptians? ye Babylonians? ye Philistines? Idolatry and arrogance toward the true God—the worship of creation instead of the Creator. And how did you reap? Your brilliant civilizations crumbled one by one. Your disposition to folly, demonstrated in Ham's revelry at his father's nakedness and in Pharaoh's obstinance toward Israel's God, led to human sacrifices and ignorance and destroyed cultures that then sank into generations of superstition.

What is it that you sowed, Abraham? Aided and abetted by your wife in your lapse of faith, you lay with Hagar, who bore you a son. And how has the reaping been? Four millennia of bloodshed and strife between the son of promise and the child of your disobedience, who even now slay each other in the name of God.

What is that you have sown, America? Genocide of the Red man, slavery of the Black man, napalming of the Yellow man; the Hollywood ethic in marriage, and the epicurean ethic in society at large. And how do you reap? Your families have shattered, your crime rate is uncontrollable, your politicians are corrupt, your children are violent, your mental disease is rampant, and your society is disordered, distorted, decadent, and diseased. You have sown to the wind and are reaping the whirlwind.

The lessons are clear. The consequences that surround us are but the logical result of our own choices. With individuals, with societies it is as the Scriptures state: "Righteousness exalteth a nation: but sin is a reproach to any people" (Prov. 14:34), and "Whatsoever a man soweth, that shall he also reap."

There is yet, however, a third way to view our text. We have learned so far that *"whatsoever* a man soweth, *that* shall he also reap."

By these we have witnessed the nature of the sowing and the character of the harvest. Now we wish to view a third perspective—the certainty of the reaping. Our text states, *"Whatsoever* a man soweth, *that shall* he also reap." Shall is different from will, or might, or may. It is not conjecture or projection or subjunctive possibility—it is imperative promise, definite future. "Whatsoever a man soweth, that *shall* he also reap."

How certain is the harvest? *Absolutely* certain! The prophetess puts it this way: "In the laws of God in nature, effect follows cause with unerring certainty. The reaping will testify as to what the sowing has been" (*Christ's Object Lessons*, p. 84).

"Intellectual power, physical stamina, and length of life depend upon immutable laws. Nature's God will not interfere to preserve men from the consequences of violating nature's requirements" (*Messages to Young People*, p. 242).

That God works no miracle to avert the harvest of our sowing is dramatically brought out in the life of King David. Under his leadership the kingdom of Israel had risen to unprecedented greatness—clearly fulfilling the covenant promises given to Abraham and Moses centuries prior.

His rule made Israel a mighty people, feared and respected among the nations. He reigned with power and acclaim. But he sinned, especially in the matter of Bathsheba. God did not cease to love him or summarily remove him from being king—but, oh, how he suffered for his mistake!

The God who repeatedly intervened to deliver him from the wrath of Saul could not—would not—protect him from the natural results of his error. Pricked to the heart by Nathan's rebuke, he confessed and repented with bitter tears, but he reaped a baleful harvest from the seeds that he had already strewn.

What was that harvest? The child of his lust died. His firstborn, Amnon, lay with his half sister. Another son, Absalom, slew Amnon and then rebelled against his father. David's trusted general, Joab, slew Absalom against David's will. Still later Adonijah, another son, rose up in insurrection as revolution and counterrevolution became commonplace in David's troubled kingdom.

The lesson we need to remember is that David's problems were not so much punishment from God as the logical consequences of his own actions. His sincere repentance did not prevent the harvest of his sowing. With saint or sinner, friend or foe—whether to the spirit or the flesh, whether immediately or at some future time—it is an irrefutable, inflexible, infallible law of God and nature that there will be "payday someday" and that "whatsoever a man soweth, that *shall* he also reap"!

To our parents in Eden the tempter urged, "Eat of the fruit, and you will live and never die." To our Saviour on Calvary he whispered, "Drink of that cup? You will die and never live." The first Adam succumbed to his doubts and brought upon us misery, while the Second Adam overcame His doubts—His fear of eternal separation from His Father—and marched on to Calvary.

His lacerated body was the seed sown in the furrows of the sepulcher, where for three days He lay dormant in death. The righteous quality of the sowing bore its logical fruitage, and the body, buried on Friday, sprang forth on Sunday—initiating an unspeakably glorious harvest.

Jesus rose, retaining His human identity, forever linked with His earthly family. The earthquake that shattered the tombs about Him yielded a wave sheaf that accompanied Him to glory as "earnests"—the firstfruits of the final harvest.

History rightly viewed is the preparation for the last glorious day when the sowing of our Saviour shall be rewarded. He is coming again to glean the earth. He has vowed and will pay, promised and will fulfill.

And it must be—for He has sown the seeds of salvation with His own blood-stained hands, and in His unfailing word is His quintessential promise: "Be not deceived; God is not mocked: for *whatsoever* a man soweth, *that shall* he also reap"!

Chapter 9

"THOU SHALT LOVE THE LORD THY GOD . . . WITH ALL THY MIND"

"And thou shalt love the Lord thy God with all thy heart, and with all thy soul, and with all thy mind, and with all thy strength: this is the first commandment" (Mark 12:30).

Each part of this fourfold command is essential for salvation. We must love God with our total heart or will, with our total soul or emotions, with our total mind or faculty of thought, and with total energy or effort. However, it is the first focus—loving the Lord with all one's mind, or with the complete potential of our intellectual faculties—that I wish to emphasize today.

The mind is as every science or psychology student can tell us, a grayish-pink object about the size of two clenched fists, comprised of connecting fibers and nerve cells known as white matter and gray matter. It has two major divisions, or hemispheres, and its surface (cortex) is roughly convoluted, giving it a wrinkled appearance. It is the stem portion of the spinal column, and the center of control for all conscious and unconscious activity.

The ancients believed that the seat of intelligence was somewhere other than the brain, ascribing this capacity in various times to the stomach, the gall bladder, the liver, and the heart. It is only recently that we have fully recognized the primacy of the brain to bodily function.

In fact, with the increase of heart transplants more and more the moment of death is being defined not as the time when the heart stops beating, but when the brain ceases to function. Contrary to what our elders believed, the brain—not the heart—is the central organ of human existence.

The brain coordinates and controls all five senses. The seat of sensation and motor control, it assembles, sorts, and interprets data as well as stores information for future use.

But more important than understanding the biological operation of the brain is our need to appreciate its role in our spiritual life and why and how we must love the Lord with all its capacity. The first reason concerns our ultimate judgment.

The essential question at the end of life's journey will not be what rules we broke or how well we achieved in comparison with others, but rather how well we utilized whatever gifts God gave us. God wants us to develop our opportunities, and He will judge our stewardship accordingly.

You know, of course, that we utilize only a portion of our mental potential. Our brains are like computers whose capacity is always far greater than we ever call upon.

Loving the Lord with all our mind is being dissatisfied with a lesser level of competence. It is activating unused gray matter—awakening dormant cells of the brain and enjoying new powers of memory and perception.

When Jesus commands "Thou shalt love the Lord thy God with all thy mind," He's not saying "Now, you sit there and think about God as hard as you can." What He really means is: "I have given you this tremendous and wonderful reasoning and thinking capacity, and I want you to develop it to the fullest of your ability. Then I will know that by this very act you will demonstrate and fulfill your love for your Creator."

A second reason for obeying this command is that each individual step up the ladder of intellectual development is a step closer to the stature from which humanity has fallen.

The essence of religion is restoration—not rule keeping. True religion is moving as far as possible toward our Edenic or original state of spiritual and mental performance. Six thousand years of disease and disobedience have sharply reduced the mental level of the human race.

Our modern-day prophet, Ellen White, has reminded us that "There perished in the Flood greater inventions of art and human skill than the world knows today. The arts destroyed were more than the boasted arts of today" (*The SDA Bible Commentary*, Ellen G. White Comments, vol. 1, p. 1089).

The inventions of our era do not demonstrate this age's superior intellect. Rather they show partial usage at least of the accumulated wisdom of the centuries. We are, in reality, intellectual pygmies standing upon the shoulders of the giants of yesteryear. Like little Jack Horner, we stick our prideful thumb into the pie of knowledge prepared by our predecessors, then with the satisfaction of each bite congratulate ourselves.

The increase of knowledge that Scripture predicts for the last days and which we enjoy is not an increase in brain power but the fortuitous discovery and utilization of prior information.

If the situation were reversed and the minds of antiquity could function with a stock of knowledge as vast as that which we have inherited, their achievements would be infinitely greater than ours.

Viewed in this light, our text reminds us that we must individually seek to arrest the decay, to halt the erosion of the powers with which we were created, and to push back toward our Edenic beginnings. We cannot expect—this far removed from creation—to approximate humanity's primal mentality. But we must try if we would please God and obey His command to love Him with full intensity.

The third reason for obeying this command is that the more of the universe we understand, the better we comprehend its Creator. "Rightly understood, science and the Written Word agree, and each sheds light on the other. Together they lead us to God" (*Counsels to Parents and Teachers*, p. 426).

The genuine scientist does not peer into the secrets of creation without being aware of the fingerprints of God. No wonder our prophet wrote, "The truths of the Divine Word can best be appreciated by an *intellectual* Christian" (*ibid.*, p. 361; italics supplied).

Tragically, some among us fear higher education, believing that loss of faith is the inevitable consequence of stellar academic endeavor. Having no curiosity about history or the cosmos, they limit their horizons to the everyday scene of their narrow worlds. They think that faith and ignorance go hand in hand and that understanding is an enemy to belief.

But every branch of knowledge rightly understood will reflect God's character. Chemistry, biology, physics, and anatomy display His creative and sustaining powers. Business and secretarial science speak of His exactness. Law reminds us of His justice and mercy. History declares His wisdom and will. Music and art tell of the beauty of His love as well as of His love of beauty. Home economics speaks of His caring and spontaneity, psychology His creative genius, sociology His uniformity, language His stunning diversity, and nursing His healing forgiveness. To expand one's mental universe is not to depreciate one's love of God—rather, it heightens our awe and intensifies our faith.

We can expand the mind and develop our intellect in two different ways. One is to feed it information that increases our mental stock and stretches our perceptual horizons. The other is to grapple with problems and concepts and thus strengthen our reasoning and decision-making. The first activity involves education—both formal and informal. We acquire formal education through organized, disciplined study. Informal education is the nonclassroom study we do—the private reading of books or personal research and writing of any kind as well as the countless things we learn from daily life.

Al Smith, a famous New York politician of the 1930s, once ran for governor of that state. A reporter at a banquet asked him, "Mr. Smith, from what university did you graduate?"

The candidate replied, "SFM."

"Let's see. SFM? I'm sorry, Mr. Smith, but what university is that?" the reporter courteously asked.

"Oh, that's Smith's Fish Market," came the reply. "That's where I learned everything I know."

The truth is that the governor hadn't been to any school of higher learning. But at his father's New York fish market he had learned the qualities of dependability, exactness, and interpersonal relationships that provided him the ingredients of success.

Students, I don't offer you SFM as an alternative to Oakwood College, but I wish to remind you that most of us could do much more to expand our mental faculties if we would make proper use of our learning opportunities in the everyday school of life.

Waiting on planes, relaxing in bed, or flying across the country all provide excellent times to read a good book or listen to good music or informative lectures. And don't forget, television offers more than sports, soaps, and situation comedies. Most cities have an excellent educational channel. Try it—you are certain to learn more from a half hour viewing the cultural highlights of Europe, or the Far East, or Afro-American history than you are likely to gain from many hours of mindless laughter, glued to some very forgettable sitcom.

Staring zombielike at valueless novels or riveting oneself for hours on end before sports events has greater potential for reducing than expanding your mind.

As for the process of formal education, I recognize that a few among us have expectations for an imminent "time of trouble" that makes sitting in a classroom for four years seem a waste of time.

Such individuals tell us that we should be eating roots and camping in the rocks and mountains as a preparation for what is to come. For them, accreditation is an unholy danger, public relations is creeping compromise, and the church is remiss in spending so many millions in support of its system of formal higher education when the end is upon us. I recognize that they are a small minority in our midst, but they are here.

And while we might use many sophisticated arguments to support the formal education that our church maintains, I wish to put it most practically by saying that when my tooth hurts I need a real doctor—not a farmer or woodsman or even a preacher, for that matter. I prefer in such cases someone whose specialty is root canals to someone whose background is root survival.

But on an even more sober plane, may I remind you who are now undergoing the process of education that you really do not have to, nor should you, wait until you have received your degree to begin working for the Lord.

Our prophet was truly inspired when she said, "Students cannot afford to wait until their education is considered complete, before using for the good of others that which they have received. Without this, however they may study, however much knowledge they may gain, their education will be incomplete" (*ibid.*, p. 263).

In other words, education and service should go hand in hand. There is no excuse for dropping out of school to "finish the work." When we work as we learn, we are even better prepared when we complete the formal education process.

A number of things can hinder our intellectual development. Among the more dangerous are: 1. *Improper eating habits.* Eating freely of sweets, eating flesh foods, eating between meals, and eating late at night will all retard mental growth by interfering with the blood supply to the brain. 2. *Lack of physical exertion.* Physical inactivity depresses mental health by restricting the oxygen flow that results from proper respiration. 3. *Lack of rest and relaxation.* Failure to "come aside and rest" now and then stunts intellectual development because overwork saps our energy reserves and paralyzes our nerves. 4. *Unstructured study habits.* Failure to have special times and places for study retards intellectual growth by encouraging laziness and distraction.

One practical but effective spur to mental vigor, believe it or not, is the daily bath—especially one concluded with a cool or cold rinse. Other more cerebral activities are memory exercises and, most important, daily study of the Word of God. Concerning this latter benefit, our prophet wrote:

"The Bible is the best book in the world for giving intellectual culture. Its study taxes the mind, strengthens the memory, and sharpens the intellect more than the study of all the subjects that human philosophy embraces" (*Gospel Workers*, p. 100).

So there you have it, scholars and teachers. I challenge you to make this school year the best of your career. Determine now at the outset that you will strive to your limit to advance as far as you can.

And, teachers, I challenge you—pour it on! Study your students. Personally motivate them toward the heights to which we beckon. Deny no student what he or she earns, but at the same time don't give anyone what he or she does not deserve. Prepare well. Explain thoroughly. And demand quality results.

It's all part of God's plan for our symmetrical development and the fulfillment of our Saviour's mandate when He said, "Thou shalt love the Lord thy God with all thy mind."

What will be the result of all this?

First, we will experience the thrill of an ever-expanding universe.

Second, we will find to our delight that we will be more efficient in everything we do.

The difference in the influence of the labors of Peter, who wrote two books of the Bible, and Paul, who wrote 13 and enjoyed a much wider scale of ministry, was not consecration or dedication—it was preparation!

"If placed under the control of His Spirit, the more thoroughly the intellect is cultivated, the more effectively it can be used in the service of God. The uneducated man who is consecrated to God . . . can be, and is, used by the Lord in His service. But those who, with the same spirit of consecration, have had the benefit of a thorough education, can do a much more extensive work for Christ. They stand on vantage ground" (*Christ's Object Lessons*, p. 333).

Third, our intellectual ability will be a glowing testimony to God's greatness. As with Daniel and his companions in Babylon, our faces should radiate with the light of His presence. Our scholarship, our research, and our instruction should testify of a superior source and presence.

Bob, the foreman of a construction company, fell in love with the boss's daughter. In fact, he proposed marriage, and to his delight obtained the approval of her family. Not long after setting the wedding date, Bob received his first major building assignment from his prospective father-in-law. For the first time since joining the firm, he was to independently supervise building a house. Imagine his enthusiasm at such an excellent opportunity to impress the boss! And with this in mind, he did everything he could to cut costs and to finish the building as quickly as he could.

Saving as much as possible on the size and quality of the foundation, he also ordered second- and third-grade lumber and paint for the partitions and the walls. Besides using the cheapest plumbing fixtures he could find, he reduced the size of the house a few feet here and there and ordered rugs that looked good but that he knew wouldn't last.

He seeded the lawn with a common grass, and having finished in record time and with substantial savings, proudly turned the keys and the balance of the money allotted for the project over to his prospective father-in-law. "Congratulations, my boy," said the boss, "but you keep the keys. The house is my wedding present to you and our daughter."

Ladies and gentlemen, you are now building the house of your lives. You will have to live in that house as long as time lasts for you. Therefore, don't cheat yourselves. Make your foundation deep and broad. Put in only quality stuff. You are the architect and builder of your own destiny. Your guarantee of success is the blueprint of the Word of God, and your chances for heaven are indelibly entwined with your willingness to follow our Lord's command.

Heaven itself will be a school. Its dual studies will be the universe and the plan of salvation. God Himself is the teacher, and through eternity He will instruct us in the mysteries of creation. "There every power will be developed, every capability increased. The grandest enterprises will be carried forward, the loftiest aspirations will be reached, the highest ambitions realized. And still there will arise new heights to surmount, new wonders to admire, new truths to comprehend, fresh objects to call forth the powers of body and mind and soul" (*Education*, p. 307).

But the chief joy of our study will not be the mysteries of the cosmos. It will be the wonder of Calvary—the inexhaustible love of Christ. There we shall sit at His feet and revel in the presence of Him who is absolute knowledge and total love. There we shall have the never-ending satisfaction of life with Him who said, "Thou shalt love the Lord thy God with all thy mind."

Chapter 10

THE POSSIBLE IMPOSSIBILITY

"Be ye therefore perfect, even as your Father which is in heaven is perfect" (Matt. 5:48).

Really, now, is there anyone among us who can truthfully claim this level of spiritual attainment? Which one of us can say that we have completely overcome Satan's power? The standard of perfection demanded by Christ in our text always beckons us higher. Not only do we humans—even the converted kind—fail to attain the *absolute* perfection or *total* godliness required in Matthew 5:48, most of us are far short of the lower plane of *relative* perfection, as well.

Was this not the kernel of Paul's plaintive confession: "I count not myself to have apprehended: but . . . I press toward the mark"?

And is this not the essence of his admission of doing what he did not want to do and not doing that which he really intended to do (Rom. 7:15-20)?

And if that is not enough to discourage any boasting of absolute perfection, consider the prophet's words: "The Lord requires no less of the soul now than He required of Adam in Paradise before he fell—perfect obedience, unblemished righteousness" (*Selected Messages*, book 1, p. 373).

Yet, since Matt. 5:48 is a promise (*Christ's Object Lessons*, p. 333), since no stain of sin will exist in the rarefied atmosphere of glory, since our characters are the only thing we will take from this world to that one, and since John did see an innumerable host of us rejoicing there, there must be a way to attain this unattainable goal—a way to make possible this seeming impossibility. But how? What is the solution to this seemingly unresolvable dilemma?

The first step toward a solution is understanding that God has given each human being the ability to make decisions. This ability, revealed in the Bible and discussed by philosophers and theologians through the centuries, functions for individual spirituality much as the parts of any machine do in its operation.

Go On!

The quality of our moral machinery determines the quality of our decisions. It was precisely this that the prophet had in mind when she wrote: "God would have His servants become acquainted with the moral machinery of their own hearts" (*Testimonies*, vol. 4, p. 85).

Of what does the human moral machinery consist? Three elements: the *appetite* or bodily urges referred to in Scripture as lusts (Gal. 5:16, 17); the *reason* (Isa. 1:18); and the *will* or determination Paul refers to in Romans 7:18. Ellen White outlines the critical role that the first two elements play in our moral success: "How . . . important that the Christian, whose eternal interests are at stake, bring appetite and passion under subjection to reason" (*The Acts of the Apostles*, p. 311). And again: "It was God's design that reason should rule the appetites, and that they should minister to our happiness" (*Temperance*, p. 12).

The third element—the will—is clearly the most important in determining moral activity. Consider the following: "But you must remember that your will is the spring of all your actions" (*Testimonies*, vol. 5, p. 515). "Everything depends upon the right action of the will" (*Steps to Christ*, p. 47). "The will is not the taste or the inclination, but it is the deciding power which works . . . unto obedience to God" (*Testimonies*, vol. 5, p. 513).

The root cause of our moral dilemma—our inability to live perfect lives—is that our moral machinery functions with faulty parts. We are born that way (Ps. 51:5). We come into the world with perverted tastes, skewed reasoning, and flabby wills. Because of this, the carnal nature is incapable of perfection.

But what do we do when the machinery is faulty? We take it to a technician who can repair or remake it. And we have all the more confidence if we go to the one who made it in the first place—the manufacturer.

So it is with our spiritual apparatus. We must take it to the One who made us, who fashioned us in His own image, and whose standards we break when we sin. Because, as His Word declares: "Neither is there salvation in any other: for there is none other name under heaven given among men, whereby we must be saved" (Acts 4:12), we have no other options. There is no shopping around for other sources of remedy.

There in the laboratory of salvation, the Holy Spirit—God's unfailing Artisan—fashions for us the clean heart and new spirit that David sought so plaintively (Ps. 51:10). God gives us new moral equipment—not overhauled or cosmetically treated, but re-created, reformed, and refocused to function with joy in the things of Christ.

What then results is what we know as the new life. Appetite, reason, and will are all revitalized, reconstituted, and reoriented toward obedience. The miracle of John 3:5 overcomes the reality of Romans 8:7.

The Possible Impossibility

Ellen White is very specific about the renewed condition of our moral equipment. 1. "When a man is converted to God, a new moral taste is created" (*Review and Herald*, June 21, 1892). 2. "It is God's purpose that the kingly power of sanctified reason, controlled by divine grace, shall bear sway in the lives of human beings" (*Messages to Young People*, p. 134). 3. "By yielding up your will to Christ, your life will be hid with Christ. . . . You will have strength from God that will hold you fast to His strength; and a new light, even the light of living faith, will be possible to you" (*Testimonies*, vol. 5, p. 514).

Only one who has had such an experience can know the unsurpassed joy of finding and following Christ.

Forgiveness, optimism, confidence, and joy unspeakable—in short, life's choicest, most rewarding benedictions—now flow like living water upon what once was a dry, barren heart, and the machinery that formerly sputtered and failed in climbing the high hills of moral obedience now responds with fresh power and moral satisfaction.

We now have joy where once we had guilt, happiness and self-worth where once we had hopelessness and self-depreciation, and the light of love where once dwelt the miasma of cynicism, greed, and the abusive titillations of corporeal desire.

Conversion is life's grandest, highest, happiest experience, but it does not allow us to claim perfection. That is because even though "all may now obtain holy hearts, . . . it is not correct to claim in this life to have holy flesh" (*Selected Messages*, book 2, p. 32).

Contrary to what many expect, conversion does not endow us with absolute righteousness. It does not rid the individual of one's carnal nature. While it sets in motion forces that allow one to resist its urgings, those urgings never cease.

Nor does conversion abolish the sinful nature. Instead it establishes within the citadel of evil (the flesh) an opposing force (the will and the mind of Christ) that preempts the flesh's formerly uncontested supremacy.

Thus despite the new spiritual and moral machinery, the Christian will often experience defeats for which he or she will need forgiveness and repentance. The process of sanctification—growing more like Christ—is inevitably accompanied by the need for justification, or the forgiveness of our sins.

But that is not a matter of discouragement. For "The closer you come to Jesus, the more faulty you will appear in your own eyes; for your vision will be clearer, and your imperfections will be seen in broad and distinct contrast to His perfect nature" (*Steps to Christ*, p. 64).

But if that is true, do we not find ourselves impaled upon the horns of an inextricable dilemma?

We know that we have been converted, that we are overcoming, but the closer to the light of Christ we advance, the more clearly we see our defects, the more obvious our unrighteousness, the more uncomfortable we are with any claim to sinless perfection.

Finally, if we are honest, we come to confess that no matter how long our Christian journey has been, we still have more ground up ahead to conquer and to realize that eternity here would be too short a span for us to develop the absolute as-your-Father-which-is-in-heaven perfection demanded in Matthew 5:48.

What, then, is the solution? How do we solve the riddle of life's possible impossibility?

Isaiah 61:10 assists us:

"I will greatly rejoice in the Lord, my soul shall be joyful in my God; for he hath clothed me with the garments of salvation, he hath covered me with the robe of righteousness, as a bridegroom decketh himself with ornaments, and as a bride adorneth herself with her jewels."

And *Christ's Object Lessons*, page 311, also helps:

"Only the covering which Christ Himself has provided can make us meet to appear in God's presence. This covering, the robe of His righteousness, Christ will put upon every repenting, believing soul."

There it is. Conversion does not render us absolutely perfect, but we are *regarded* as so because we wear the robe of His righteousness.

Now it can be said of us as it was of Abraham:

"He staggered not at the promise of God through unbelief; but was strong in faith, giving glory to God; and being fully persuaded that, what he had promised, he was able also to perform. And therefore it was imputed to him for righteousness" (Rom. 4:20-22).

The Father's judgment focuses on Christ's robe—our covering—and not our internal condition.

True, that condition is vastly improved in comparison to our preconversion state, but the carnal flesh still remains, tempting us to sins of omission and excess.

While the strength of those urges has reduced in proportion to our diligence in studying God's Word, the body of sin, be it ever so weak, still sends to our minds a never-ending stream of evil desire to stain our spiritual credibility and spoil our hope of absolute perfection.

Christ's righteous robe superimposed upon us—not a perfect body but a struggling soul covered by the robe of Christ—is seen by God as an acceptable arrangement for our redemption.

It is thus that we are able to meet the absolute requirements of Matthew 5:48.

This marvelous fact of salvation was never more succinctly expressed than in the words of Ellen White who exclaimed, "Thank God we are not dealing with impossibilities. We may claim sanctification. We may enjoy the favor of God. We are not to be anxious about what Christ and God think of us, but about what God thinks of Christ, our Substitute" (*Selected Messages*, book 2, pp. 32, 33).

This fact makes friendship with Christ the most vital of life's activities. Heaven's joys outshine the transient pleasures of this life's brief span as the sun does the firefly.

There no stain of evil can enter—no blight of sin, no nuance of transgression. "Iniquity shall not rise the second time!"

The change from corruption to incorruption at the Second Coming will be the harmonizing at last of our corporeal selves with our spiritual wills. We will lose these bodies of sin—these dynamos of evil that have so long transmitted signals of lust and temptation to disobey.

At last we shall be free—perfectly tuned to the will of God and perfectly adapted to His will, as innocent and unsullied as were Adam and Eve before they fell.

I must be there. You must be there. We can, and we will if we will seek and accept the promises of perfection available in the righteousness of His redeeming life.

The hymnist's words capture the essence of our need and its only resolution:

> Look upon Jesus, sinless is He;
> Father, impute His life unto me.
> My life of scarlet, my sin and woe,
> Cover with His life, whiter than snow.
>
> Cover with His life, whiter than snow;
> Fullness of His life then shall I know;
> My life of scarlet, my sin and woe,
> Cover with His life, whiter than snow.

Chapter 11

"ME AND MY HOUSE"

"And if it seem evil unto you to serve the Lord, choose you this day whom ye will serve; whether the gods which your fathers served that were on the other side of the flood, or the gods of the Amorites, in whose land ye dwell; but as for me and my house, we will serve the Lord" (Joshua 24:15).

Joshua the proud and regal warrior is standing before the people for the last time. Three decades of judging the tribes and 30 major campaigns of war have dimmed neither his eye nor his voice. But they do reflect in the lines creasing his face and the white of his hair. And today he is unusually solemn. God has told him that he is about to die.

This, his farewell sermon, is not long, as sermons go—in fact, it encompasses less than 26 verses of the final chapter of the book that bears his name. It is nostalgic but it is also comprehensive. His sermon covers the glories of Israel's past, highlighting military victories and the wilderness miracles whereby God had led His people.

But the highlight of this speech is none of these events. It is neither the triumph of the Red Sea nor the time when the sun stood still nor the crumpling of the walls of Jericho. Rather, it is the warning against family dissolution given in the text above—the recognition of a trend that more than any other threatened the social and spiritual welfare of God's people. Joshua saw that God's people were adopting the family customs of their heathen neighbors and that this apostasy was muting their spirituality and undermining their national will and purpose.

Such is always the effect of family breakdown. No nation, no group, is stronger than the parts that make up the whole.

What more than any other cause has rendered the Black race in America so susceptible to crime, illegitimacy, illiteracy, and a culture of poverty and second-class values? The devastation of our family system wrought by 300 years of American slavery.

The first blows to Black family solidarity were struck when slavers snatched our forbearers from their homes in Africa. That process intensified when the captives were bartered as soulless beasts at auction blocks on the shores of the Americas and worsened in captivity as men became drones and women the sex objects of lustful owners.

Thus, was the foundation laid for the generations of social disorder that have followed.

The reasons differ but what is true of the Black family unit is true of America in general. That which has more than anything else marked the moral decline of our nation is the collapse of our family institution.

America the beautiful? What's so beautiful about 20,000 people dying on the highways each year from alcohol-related accidents? What's so beautiful about 25,000 murders each year? Or drug traffic of epidemic proportions? Or crime rate? Or the 1.2 million divorces annually in our nation—not to mention the animosity and bitterness that grip a significant percentage of those who do not divorce? What's so beautiful about 30,000 suicides every year? And what's so beautiful about lying politicians, dishonest judges, extorting police officers, fornicating clergy, embezzling bankers, and bribe-taking athletes?

Sin is the cause, you say. Of course—and sin flourishes most with populations made weak by family disorganization. Society is most vulnerable to character ills when the home—the factory that produces the leaders and citizens of the community—breaks down.

Our spouse swappings, multiple marriages, quickie divorces, burgeoning illegitimacy, and rampant promiscuity all demonstrate a sick society—a virtueless citizenry spawned by a family system gone wrong.

Very much a cause of our family decline is our unhealthy courtship pattern—the most unsuccessful form of contracting marriage there is.

We 250 million Americans have more divorces and separations than the other 5.3 billion earthlings put together. It's humbling to note that even those cultures where marriage is contracted by dowery or even by capture have higher marital success than ours.

The brute truth is that the American family system today is a bankrupt institution—destroyed by unfaithful spouses, insensitive fathers, angry wives, unbridled children, and premarital and extramarital sex. All these have brought us to a state of cesspool degeneracy from which it appears impossible to escape.

But my primary focus is not upon the godless society about us but upon us as members of the household of faith—modern Israelites, that is. And I want to preface what follows with this statement:

"Many seem to think that the declension in the church, the growing love of pleasure, is due to want of pastoral work. True, the church is to be provided with faithful guides and pastors. Ministers should labor earnestly for the youth who have not given themselves to Christ, and also for others who, though their names are on the church roll, are irreligious and Christless. But ministers may do their work faithfully and well, yet it will amount to very little if parents neglect their work. It is to a lack of Christianity in the home life that the lack of power in the church is due" (*Child Guidance*, p. 550).

We give a lot of reasons that the church is not experiencing Pentecost or the falling of the latter rain. Some blame our lengthy wilderness wanderings on our conference officials, accusing them of politics and fiscal mismanagement. Others lay the blame on our pastors, blaming them for insensitivity, shallow sermonizing, and "quickie" baptisms. Many attack our schools, seeing them as too soft on standards, etc.

But in fact the real problem is none of the above. The most persuasive deterrent to our accomplishing the gospel commission is not the church houses or the school house, but *our* houses—the places where we live.

What the church needs more than new pastors and better schools is more parents who love the Lord, who are determined that "the line shall not break 'where they stand,'" and who are willing to say like Joshua: "Choose you this day whom ye will serve; . . . but as for me and my house, we will serve the Lord" (Joshua 24:15).

If our homes are to fulfill God's purposes, we need not only to be aware of the above but also have a working knowledge of the principles and practices of successful families. These principles, freely enunciated in the Word of God and the writings of Ellen White, are more important to our individual happiness than all the "how to" books on marriage that one sees on the market.

The information that inspiration provides us is detailed and clear. Faithful regard for such counsel will arm one with techniques that guide from the first "hello" of acquaintance to the "I do" at the altar, on to "It's a boy" or "It's a girl" at childbirth, to the "All right, you can have the car—just be careful" at teenage, to the "Hi, Dad, how's Mom?" during college days, to "dust to dust and ashes to ashes at the goodbye"—or from boy meets girl "till death do us part."

Want to know the important qualities to look for in a prospective mate? Then read *Adventist Home*, and observe that the primary qualities one should seek in a wife are those of patience, selflessness, economizing, and efficiency in practical duties (pp. 45, 46).

And the same source gives the main qualities that a woman should seek in a husband. They are diligence, honesty, self-motivation, and respect for his mother (*ibid.*, pp. 47, 48). Included in the counsel of our prophet regarding courtship is caution against keeping late hours (*Messages to Young People*, pp. 457, 458), against being too frequently together (*ibid.*, p. 438), the dangers of listening to sentimentally suggestive music (*ibid.*, p. 295), and any physical contact that may break down the barriers of modesty (*The Adventist Home*, pp. 55-60).

The prophet also speaks against making plans for marriage without consultation with and approval of parents (*ibid.*, p. 458). She condemns engagements that are too short as to deny ample time for thorough acquaintance. But on the other hand, she discourages engagements that last so long as to intensify temptations to impropriety (*ibid.*, pp. 55-57).

But that is not all. The specifics of divine counsel include instruction as to where to live—away from the crowded cities (*ibid.*, pp. 131-147); the type of furniture to purchase—simple but sturdy (*ibid.*, p. 150); the frequency of childbearing—the emphasis being on the health of the mother and the financial capacity of the parents (*ibid.*, p. 162ff); and the dominant role of the parents—the father being the priest, protector, and provider and the mother, the homemaker and chief guide for the children (*ibid.*, pp. 212-232).

Instructions throughout the book provide an illuminating list of child-rearing techniques involving discipline, companionship, recreation, worship, education, and even our obligations to care for our aging parents.

And through it all, one constant reminder prevails—the only honorable way for a marriage to dissolve is in death.

Annulment, separation, and divorce are all unfortunate interruptions of a marital relationship. Even when biblically approved, their effect debilitates our children and society. Marriage is a lifetime contract. Those of us who are still single need to understand that. And those of us already married need to remember that and to reaffirm daily that no matter what others may do or what course society may take, "as for me and my house, we will serve the Lord."

Other young people may pet and party and engage in premarital sex, but as for me and my friend, "we will serve the Lord."

Other parents may permit records, books, magazines, novels, music, and TV programs displaying pornography and lovesick sentimentalism, but "as for me and my house, we will serve the Lord."

Other parents may become discouraged and send their children to schools where they will experience unsanctified philosophies, ungodly examples, and undesirable social pressures, but "as for me and my house, we will serve the Lord."

Other families may attend divine worship services spasmodically and Sabbath school and youth activities almost never, but "as for me and my house, we will serve the Lord."

Go On!

Other families may rush out into the busy world each morning without singing a song, reading Scripture, and kneeling in a prayer of consecration, but "as for me and my house, we will serve the Lord."

We will serve Him when we cannot see or understand the circumstances that engulf us, and we will serve Him through whatever clouds of difficulty or tragedy sweep over us.

Always we will beam in on the radar of His Holy Word, knowing that He is faithful to His promises.

Even when human logic seems to dictate a different route, we will serve Him because we trust Him and believe that "all His biddings are enablings" and that "all things work together for good to them that love God." Today, tomorrow, and as long as He gives us breath we will serve Him.

Our Lord documented His concern for our homes during His life on earth. He performed His first miracle at a wedding reception, healed the centurion's servant, raised Jairus' daughter, healed Peter's mother-in-law, raised the widow's only child, sent the Gadarian demoniacs back to their families fully restored, transplanted the lepers from their colony of outcasts to their joyous loved ones, and glorified family communion by sharing the residence of Mary, Martha, and Lazarus. His final words upon the cross included a tender expression for His mother.

Christ is as eager now as He was then to bless our homes. That is why we can with confidence and resolve mirror the awareness and the determination of that ancient warrior, Joshua, who, in circumstances very much like ours, rose to the challenge with unshakable commitment and stoutly proclaimed, "As for me and my house, we will serve the Lord"!

Chapter 12

"I Am That I Am"

"And Moses said unto God, Behold, when I come unto the children of Israel, and shall say unto them, The God of your fathers hath sent me unto you; and they shall say to me, What is his name? what shall I say unto them? And God said unto Moses, I AM THAT I AM: and he said, Thus shalt thou say unto the children of Israel, I AM hath sent me unto you" (Ex. 3:13, 14).

Imagine the scene—Moses has just completed not four but 40 years of graduate studies in the University of Sinai. Don't misunderstand, it wasn't that he was slow. His degree attainments in Egypt had already proved that he was, in fact, quite a scholar.

Why then did it take him so long in Sinai? Well, his need was meekness, and his career, which would span 40 of the most crucial years of the plan of salvation, demanded that he have the highest of degrees—the BHG—Baptism of the Holy Ghost. And to be sure, he finally finished, but only after completing the toughest curriculum imaginable. It included a major in humility and a minor in self-abnegation.

And it worked, for later God declared that Moses was the meekest man who ever lived. But now it was time to leave. Commencement day had arrived, and with it God announced his first job assignment—and it was a "biggie"! All God wanted him to do was engineer the escape of a whole nation of hostages from Egypt.

Impossible!

First of all, Pharaoh was certain to resist with every agency at his disposal. No way would he stand by and lose all that free labor.

In the second place, the Hebrew people themselves had lost hope in deliverance and would probably laugh at the suggestion that Moses, who had been on the "Ten Most Wanted List" of Egypt for four decades, could now demand their freedom with nothing more than a rod.

No wonder Moses was frightened. It was time to be scared, and so he stands there in his bare feet by the burning bush and pleads his inability to do what God asks.

He'd much rather stay in school than go into Egypt.

"But they'll never listen," he pleads to God. "They'll never believe me. Maybe if

You give me some kind of sign—some kind of special certificate or diploma—maybe then they'll listen to me."

"Don't worry about that," God replies. "Just put your shoes on, go tell Jethro and Zipporah goodbye, and proceed down to Egypt. When you get there and they ask you who sent you, your only reply should be 'I AM THAT I AM'!"

God's pointed and in many ways elusive response, "I AM THAT I AM," given Moses at his Sinai commencement, tells us two things that I think we should especially remember today. The first has to do with the sense of God's transcendence—the "otherness" or the distance of God—that this name implies. Sometimes God has used human categories to describe Himself. Other times He has permitted humans veiled glimpses of His majesty and power. But they are necessarily incomplete revelations of His glory—not face-to-face encounters with Him who is a consuming fire.

God seldom presents Himself with lengthy introductions or detailed outlines of His credentials. But then, if He had decided to write such a résumé, could Moses really have understood it? Can finite humanity grasp the categories of infinity? It was as if God was saying to Moses, "Don't try to explain it. My qualifications exceed human comprehension. When they ask who sent you on this 'mission impossible,' just tell them, 'I AM THAT I AM.'"

Our quest for meaning has two contrary roots. The first is that of the Gentiles, which begins with the dictum "Know thyself." The problem, of course, is that those determined to know themselves before knowing God never get around to the latter. The philosopher Descartes, who saw man as a subject—the acting center of his consciousness—said, "I think—therefore, I am." When challenged with the idea that it might not be thinking that he was doing, he replied, "All right, I doubt—therefore, I am."

Hume, a later philosopher, saw humans more as objects than thinking subjects and described them as a bundle of impersonal nerves and emotions moving in endless physiological wonder—creatures being acted upon rather than initiating things themselves. Thus, while Descartes found the doubting "I," Hume saw no "I" at all, and—as in the case with all non-Christian theorists—neither was able to move beyond their humanistic musings to the reality of transcendence.

Now the Hebrews' problem was quite the opposite. They sought to comprehend divinity as a prelude to knowing humanity. However, their attempts to move from heavenly knowns to earthly unknowns were frustrated by their inability to pierce the veil that separates us from transcendence. Their dilemma is summed up in Zophar's question to Job, "Canst thou by searching find out God?" (Job 11:7). The "I AM THAT I AM" pronouncement of Exodus suggests that we cannot. Why? Because, as

"I Am That I Am"

Kant reminds us, reason gives meaning to understanding, and understanding, which interprets matter in terms of size, shape, color, and substance, can deal only with tangible things.

But God exists out of range of any of the five senses. It is true that "the heavens declare the glory of God." They do "refer" us to our Maker, but they do not allow us to squeeze Him into our categories of time and space. We simply cannot explain or comprehend this God who walks on air and who has neither beginning nor end. Our predecessors were not wrong to proclaim absolute certainty about both God's will and His ways. They were, as history attests, inaccurate in some of their prophetic interpretations and doctrinal formulations. But since they understood to the limits of their perceptual capacities, they were justified in their conclusions.

We are now, however, benefiting from the tools of higher education that have sharpened our research capacity and increased our accuracy. Those who have spent long, arduous years developing and utilizing the skills of research and critical analysis are like contemporary astronomers who view the skies through new and more powerful lenses. These scientists look at the same heavens as their progenitors, but they see more stars and chart more stellar beauty. Thus armed with the aids that scholarship provides, we are increasingly uncomfortable with those sermons we hear and those articles we read that are the products of shoddy or shallow thinking. Without doubt, when education does its work well, it sharpens our reasoning, it alters our thought processes, and it enhances our structures of belief.

But what we must remember is that our feeble rationality, no matter how well honed, cannot penetrate the world of Omnipotence. We cannot break the codes of infinity. The best we can do is view the world about us through the lens of credible scholarship and cry with Elihu, "Touching the Almighty, we cannot find Him out" (Job 37:23).

Why? Because He does not, on cue, walk out on the stage of the universe to let humanity touch and examine Him, and if He did, our intellectual equipment could not decipher Him.

It is not *sense* knowledge we have of God—it is *faith* knowledge. Such an understanding allows us to admit that our views of Him are relative and that relative knowledge about an absolute God is the only option believers can ever have. Kant was right when he saw the traditional proofs of God as threatening the need for faith. Faith is unnecessary where proof exists. Our grasping for full certainty—our attempts to lasso Deity with human cords—ignores the fact that the words of the prophets are merely symbols of divine reality, incomplete representations of incomprehensible being.

Go On!

Finite minds can never capture an infinite God.

Our encounters with transcendence are approaches to an unfathomable Being who condescends to caricature Himself in the colloquial expressions of earth. He does not speak to us in His language—He speaks in ours.

How else could we understand Him?

Viewed from this perspective, all our prattlings about who God is and what God is doing are but tentative probings into absolute mysteries.

Niebuhr was correct when he said that no matter what our conclusions, "we are all wrong." Thus, God is to the end of our lives, and to the end of the ages, the Mysterium Tremendum—a God high and lifted up, a God terrible in majesty whose ways are past finding out—a God whose résumé reads: "I AM THAT I AM."

But we are not without clues. God does give us hints that we can grasp.

In His reply, "I AM THAT I AM," we find not only His loftiness and incomprehensibility but also His loving concern and His active involvement in the human condition.

A grammatical analysis of this name reveals much that speaks to the point.

Observe it is "I" am, or the first person, in which He speaks. His will for Moses is not coming through an angel or a prophet or even in a dream—this is no secondhand party contact or mystical experience. This is Moses and God, one on one. The job is critical, Moses is His chosen instrument for success, so God does the speaking Himself. To Moses is given the highest honor possible. The highest authority in the universe interacts with him regarding his future. And He says, "Moses, don't argue with Me, don't argue with them. Tell them when they ask you 'I' am that 'I' am."

Second, notice the *voice* in which He speaks. His words are: I "*am*." This is not the passive voice, the voice of disinterest, nor is it the subject being acted upon—for God is not the subject being acted upon. He is not a passive potentate nor is He functioning as one of those absentee landlords or sterile deities "who haunt the lucid interspace of worlds above where never creeps a cloud nor moves a wind, nor ever falls the least white star of snow, nor ever lowest roll of thunder moans, nor sound of human sorrow ever mounts to mar their sacred everlasting calm." No! No! He is not passive or unperturbed. He is an involved, concerned, and acting God, and His name is "I AM THAT I AM."

Third, observe the *number* here indicated. Again His words are "I am." He speaks not simply in the first person active, but it is the first person singular in which He introduces Himself.

He could have invoked the first person plural—and He would have been correct to say "We are that We are." But He would have confused the polytheists of Egypt had He spoken in the first person plural. He spoke in the singular because He always starts with the known and moves to the unknown. And because in the end it was the fact that there was no other God but the triune one with which He wanted to impress the inhabitants of Egypt.

He desired not to be compared with their family of gods nor did He simply want to be exalted above all others, because there are *no* others. He was not to be made better than others because *no* others exist. And when He said "I am," He was speaking in the singular because He is singular, unique, and His words to Moses "I am that I am" were specifically to imply "I am" and only "I am."

Fourth, there is the *tense* in which God describes Himself. And in what tense does He proclaim "I AM THAT I AM"? It is, to coin a phrase, the "eternal present." He is not only everywhere—He is everywhen. The worshipers of Ra, Horus, Osiris, and all the other gods of Egypt humanized their deities. People gave them origins, places of birth, and even at times believed that their gods had been condemned to die. We might chart the existence of such gods with any of the usual verbal tenses—the past, *I was;* the past perfect, *I had been;* the future, *I shall be;* the future perfect, *I shall have been;* and, of course, while alive they could use the simple present, *I am.* But only the "I AM THAT I AM" can claim to encompass all of time's categories—I was; I have been; I shall have been; I am; and then conclude, I always was and I always will be—"I AM THAT I AM."

Fifth, the name "I AM THAT I AM" reflects the nearness and availability of God, and that is the fact that it is spoken in what the Hebrews labeled the causative *case.* In the final analysis, the universe has only two kinds of existence: self-existence and created existence. It is, of course, the former by which God here portrays Himself, and it is not just self-existence but creative existence that is implied as well.

The "I AM" of the burning bush reminds us here that He is "the only Cause without cause," "the first Cause," "the efficient Cause," "the Cause behind all effects," "the unmoved Mover," "the universal Unconditioned" of heaven and earth. As such, He is not to be considered in the comparative (there is no other God with comparable capacities) or in the superlative (He is not the best of the creative gods)—He is the *only* God. Thus, He can say not only "I AM" but also "I AM and only I AM," "I AM because I AM"—"I AM THAT I AM."

The sixth aspect of the verbal expression "I AM THAT I AM" helpful to our balanced view of God is its *mood.* "I AM THAT I AM" is not subjunctive, indicating probability, or indicative, that is, a simple statement of fact. It is *imperative!*

God is not presenting Himself as a celestial "perhaps" or a cosmic "maybe."

Neither is He expressing Himself simply as historical being. Rather, He uses the voice of urgency—the mood of dynamism and aggression. What He is saying to Moses is, "Let them know that something is about to happen. Tell them that while I am high and holy, I am also available and involved, and that I am about to do something dramatic, immediate, and cataclysmic in their behalf—'I AM THAT I AM.'"

And so, students, put your shoes on now—there's a vast Egypt of sickness and sin awaiting you out there. In the midst of that cauldron of evil are a lot of nice people looking for a better life, and a lot of confused people crippled by intemperance and hardened by cynicism but whose minds have not yet closed to the voice of God. Your job is to help rescue them. You must utilize your skills, your knowledge, in the greatest search and rescue mission history has known.

But I don't make any glowing promises—I don't claim that you will turn the world upside down, or even our city upside down, or even our church or school or hospital or office upside down. I don't even promise that you will finish the job in your lifetime.

I hope you do—but I can't promise that.

I don't promise immunity from disease or accident or even premature death. Nor can I promise fairness or equity or the comforts of life. It's a hard, cruel world, and membership in God's army does not exempt us from its tragedies.

But I do pledge upon the authority of God's Word that come weal or woe, sickness or health, life or death, the presence of the "I AM" will provide ultimate meaning to your existence, clear guidance in your decision-making, constant solace for your trials, and everlasting reward for your faith.

You who are going overseas as missionaries will meet with difficulties far from family, but fear not—the great "I AM" has said, "Go and I will go with you!"

You who will sell books or give Bible studies, knocking on doors in citadels of sin, will be often rebuffed, but do not despair—the "I AM" of the burning bush is the "I Will" of the concrete jungles.

You who seek higher education will struggle with theories of humanism, evolutionism, socialism, positivism, scientism, hedonism, and materialism. But hold on to your trust in God—the "I AM" of your faith is greater than the "I propose" of any human theory.

No matter where you witness—in corporate board rooms, by hospital beds, in foundation think tanks, before giant machinery—whatever, wherever, whenever, and however God guides you—you can and must function only and always in that wondrous name.

An unknown poet has appropriately written, "When God would teach mankind

"I Am That I Am"

His name He calls Himself the 'Great I AM' and leaves a blank so believers may supply those things for which they pray."

What is your need? Employment, further education, family solidarity, financial security, friendship, courage? In your hand is the check already signed "I AM THAT I AM"! It is dated at Calvary, written with the eradicable blood of Jesus. All that you need to make this gift negotiable is for you to fill in the blank—write in whatever you need and take its promises with you as you fight in the Egypt of daily life. Thus endowed and imbued by One who promises never to leave us—"No, never to leave us alone"—you will reap maximum satisfaction and reward.

Then go, beloved,

> and may the grace of Christ be before you to guide you;
> may the goodness of Christ be above you to shield you;
> may the mercy of Christ be behind you to protect you;
> may the principles of Christ be around you to mold you;
> may the promises of Christ be beside you to sustain you;
> may the love of Christ be within you to propel you;
> and underneath may there always be the everlasting arms
> of the great "I AM."

Chapter 13

"I Am Joseph"

"Then Joseph could not refrain himself before all them that stood by him; and he cried, Cause every man to go out from me. And there stood no man with him, while Joseph made himself known unto his brethren. And he wept aloud: and the Egyptians and the house of Pharaoh heard. And Joseph said unto his brethren, I am Joseph" (Gen. 45:1-3).

It had been 20 years since Joseph had seen his brothers. He had left home at the age of 17—about the time that many young people today leave home in quest of education, never to return as a permanent resident.

But his case was different.

Joseph left home on what was to have been a brief visit with his shepherd brothers.

But when they saw him coming, they decided to kill him. Why? Because he had repeatedly offended them with stories of dreams that predicted their servitude to him and because their father continued to show him unabashed favoritism. And they would have carried out their malicious intent except for the intervention of the oldest son, Reuben, who suggested that they throw him into a pit instead, and of Judah, who engineered Joseph's sale to a passing band of Ishmaelites.

At any rate, Joseph never went back home. Instead, he became a servant in Potiphar's house, where he labored for 10 lonely years.

Then came the incident with Potiphar's wife that got him thrown into prison. After three miserable years of imprisonment his facility for interpreting dreams came in handy when he interpreted Pharaoh's dream and received as reward a political appointment of unbelievable status: he was made second in command of Egypt, next to Pharaoh himself.

There for 10 exciting years he pursued a career in the most powerful nation of the then-known world. He had climbed from pit to palace—from the bottom of the well where he had been left to perish to the mountaintop of political authority.

But his success had a lingering blight. You see, becoming prime minister without your family knowing it is like a golfer making "a hole in one" when no one is looking.

Or like shooting 25 straight free throws in an empty gym.

All of us crave approbation. We all long for approval, especially from our significant others. Joseph felt that need. And in the midst of his busy activities as prime minister in Egypt he carried the pain of rejection and a longing for fellowship and reinstatement with his own.

And now, like something out of Ripley's "Believe It or Not," there they were—right there before his very eyes!

He recognized them immediately.

But since this dignitary in his late 30s bore little resemblance to the lad they had sold into slavery, they had no clue to his identity.

Joseph, however, knew every one of them—all 10—and while he remembered their treachery at Dothan, he was eager to talk with them, to inquire about his father's health and that of his only full-blooded brother, Benjamin, whom he noticed was not with them.

Was Jacob still living? Was Benjamin well? Would they accept him? Would they believe him?

And there was another problem.

What would Pharaoh think? Asiatic shepherds were a despised lot among the Egyptians. How would he and Egypt's other leaders react to these dusty foreigners?

With an excited but worried heart, Joseph reacted with humanity's most common response to such emotions of nostalgia and surprise: he cried.

Not once, not twice, but three times during this ordeal he hid himself from his brothers and wept.

He kept manipulating the circumstances, hoping for time to decide what to do.

First, he had his brothers sent back home without telling them his identity. Then when they returned, he threw a banquet in their behalf and sent them home again. But then he sent troops to intercept them and bring them back. No longer able to contain himself, he exclaimed in relief, "I am Joseph, your brother" (see Gen. 45:3).

And then while his brothers sat paralyzed with fear and surprise, Joseph cried from 20 years of bitterness, animosity, frustration, and fading hope.

Hearing the commotion, Pharaoh inquired about the situation, and being informed, ordered a huge celebration to mark the memorable event.

Joseph sent for his father, who at first dared not believe this incredible turn of events, but once entering Egypt, spent the rest of his otherwise troubled life in peace and prosperity with his rich and powerful son.

But my message to you is not about Jewish history or Egyptian culture or how to become prime minister in five easy steps. What I really want to talk about is the focus of life that the expression "I am Joseph" presents. For, you see, it contains several views of Joseph, critical not only to his relationship to his brothers but also essential to the spiritual welfare of each of us.

The first interpretation of "I am Joseph" renders him as the agent of *consequences*. The deeds of his 10 older brothers have now come home to roost. They thought the dreamer was gone—forever banished from their consciences. In fact, when their prime minister brother questioned them about their family they referred to him as the brother who "is not" (Gen. 42:13). They had written him off as forever gone and viewed their dastardly deed at Dothan as a buried secret of the past. But now here he is in undeniable reality—their brother, the prime minister of Egypt—saying, "I am Joseph."

It is thus with all of life. The directions that we take at the well of decision always resurface at the table of later years. Life is a movement from pit to palace, from cause to effect, from negotiation to remuneration, and every day is payday for some prior investment. Each result that comes to us is a grown-up consequence, bearing either smiles of satisfaction or the pain of regret as it declares, "I am Joseph."

Notice how firmly their earlier indiscretions came back to haunt them.

First, all 10 brothers had to spend three troubled days in jail—not as punishing a plight as Joseph's three years of incarceration but symbolic recompense, nevertheless, for their insensitive treatment of him two decades earlier.

Second, it was Simeon, the chief instigator in the plot to destroy Joseph, who was bound and detained at the conclusion of their initial visit (Gen. 42:24).

Third, Jacob himself suffered throughout this exchange. Jacob the deceiver, who had said "I am Esau" to trick his father and who had flimflammed his way to the birthright and material success. He too was reaping what he had sowed in his youth of deceit.

When informed after the first visit that the ruler in Egypt demanded the presence of his youngest, Benjamin, he replied in agony, "Me have ye bereaved of my children: Joseph is not, and Simeon is not, and ye will take Benjamin away: all these things are against me" (verse 36).

It is true that the wheels of justice sometimes "grind slowly but always exceedingly fine."

We do reap what we sow.

The game of life has no "rainouts," no plays called back. Sometimes in His mercy God provides a little overtime, or, as in the case of Hezekiah, a few extra innings. But the only replay is in the judgment when our deeds will be flashed back to condemn or to delight us.

Our "pit time" of sowing determines our "palace days" of reaping. What we plant in the Dothan of our youth, we will reap in the Egypt of adulthood. Each of life's decisions rises up in later judgment to declare, "I am Joseph."

But it is not only the Joseph of consequences who faces his brothers here. He is also the Joseph of *forgiveness*. If he were only the Joseph of recompense, he would have rewarded their treachery by refusing their requests, or perhaps condemned them to imprisonment and even death.

But Joseph is forgiving, and the account of Genesis 45:7-14 tells that his compassion overruled any desire for revenge—he accepted and nurtured his needy family.

They had wanted to kill him and had succeeded in selling him into slavery. Now he is in a position in which he could easily repay their evil, but instead he forgives.

However, his forgiveness was not automatic.

In fact, Joseph expressed it only after he had studied his brothers' conduct and knew that their attitudes had changed.

How could he be so sure?

He tested them—not once or twice, but four times.

First, he roughed them up. He treated them as if they were enemies of the state—accused them of being spies and put them in prison. In other words, he gave them a hard time and studied their reactions for evidence of humility and sincerity of purpose.

Second, he listened to their reaction to his demand that Benjamin be brought back upon their return. The terror that seized them during their imprisonment and the fear of Jacob's reaction to the ruler's demand caused them great pain. They discussed their plight freely (in the Hebrew language), not knowing that Joseph understood their every word (Gen. 42:23). And Joseph was impressed. He noticed their contrition and was convinced that they were genuinely sorry for what they had done.

Third, he tested them at the banquet he arranged during their second visit. The brothers were perplexed by two developments: (1) they were seated in the precise order of their birth, and (2) Benjamin, the youngest, received five times as much food as anyone else (Gen. 43:33, 34). Joseph's rationale for all this? By dramatizing the seeming inequity in favoring the youngest above the rest, he was simulating the reality of his status both in childhood and now as their potential benefactor.

They had reacted violently to his youthful dreams of their subservience—how would they respond to similar privileges given to Benjamin, his full-blooded brother, the only other son of his mother, Rachel? Had they questioned the preferential arrangements or demonstrated jealousy toward Benjamin, Joseph would have known that the selfishness that had caused the deed at Dothan still existed. But they did not respond in the old way. And again the prime minister was impressed.

Joseph's fourth test of repentance occurred when he charged them with the theft of the silver (Gen. 44:14, 16). Having apprehended them, he demanded that they leave Benjamin with him while they returned to their father. Judah's plaintive plea about the harm it would bring Jacob if they went home without Benjamin, and his offer of himself as surety or guarantee of Benjamin's return, touched Joseph's heart.

Seeing their sorrow and convinced of their remorse, he expelled all other persons from the room, and, in heavyhearted but triumphant reconciliation, confessed, "I am Joseph!"

And what kind of baggage do you bring to God's banquet table today? Are you weighted down with parcels of selfishness, envy, pride, dishonesty, lust, intemperance, or worldliness? Have you too sought to hide God's message of mercy in the pit of denial?

We have, have we not? Often we have bartered our Lord for worldly gain, have refused His pleadings, and drowned out conscience while grasping for that which satisfieth not. Refusing to obey the voice of reason and righteousness, we have lied to the Father and then have paid in terms of soiled characters, lost opportunities, wasted years, squandered talents, and sorrowing loved ones. Over and over again we have wounded our Lord.

But today acceptance and reconciliation are available. Jesus stands before us ready to forgive and to forget. The God of justice and recompense is also the God of mercy and forgiveness. "He hath not dealt with us after our sins; nor rewarded us according to our iniquities" (Ps. 103:10). Our disobedience is great, but His forgiveness is far greater. He woos us even before we know Him, and His promise to all who will accept Him is "I am Joseph."

But he is not only the Joseph of consequence and the Joseph of forgiveness, he is also the Joseph of *assurance.* Understandably, Jacob found his sons' report of their having discovered their brother alive and in command of Pharaoh's storehouse unbelievable.

He had inspected the sagging wagons bearing food and expensive gifts—but he dared not believe.

Nevertheless, finally reassured by the tangible evidences of Joseph's love, the patriarch packed all his earthly possessions and went with his sons to dwell in Egypt.

Comforted by the security of Joseph's authority and concern, Jacob spent his latter years in joyful peace and prosperity. His death, however, precipitated a final crisis for the brothers. Genesis 50:15 puts it this way: "And when Joseph's brethren saw that their father was dead, they said, Joseph will peradventure hate us, and will certainly requite us all the evil which we did unto him."

To put it simply, they were scared to death! They were afraid that Joseph had befriended them only because Jacob was alive, and now that he was dead, he would surely get his revenge.

Sadly some people serve the church or act civilly only because they fear what their parents might say as long as they are alive. Not so with Joseph. His father's death did not alter his behavior. Joseph, who forgave and accepted his brothers when Jacob was alive, maintained that posture when the old man was gone.

His reply to his brothers' trepidation was, "Fear ye not: I will nourish you, and your little ones" (Gen. 50:21). What reassurance to have one's brother, the prime minister, confidant to the king, guardian of the commissaries, pledge such a guarantee.

During my years of travel I have seen a lot of famous people at airports and other public places. They include Martin Luther King, Jr., Jimmy Carter, Pat Boone, Joe Namath, Nat King Cole, Edward Kennedy, Joe Louis, Howard K. Smith, Jackie Robinson, Howard Cosell, Jesse Jackson, Henry Aaron, Ella Fitzgerald, Colonel Sanders, Henry Kissinger, Muhammad Ali, Ronald Reagan, and others. All such encounters have been memorable, but with the exception of Martin Luther King, Jr., the one involving John F. Kennedy was the most thrilling of them all.

With the nation in general, I followed closely the excitement of Kennedy's brief tenure in office and was impressed particularly with his visit to Ireland, the land of his forebears' birth. I shall never forget the pictures that showed him being feted by the exuberant Irish. Understandably flattered by his presence, they showered him with attentions and praise as he reassured them with promises of friendship and political support.

One unforgettable photo displayed a cherubic-faced, middle-aged woman reaching out from the crowd with a smile of adoration. The caption quoted her as saying, "Ireland will never worry again. Our boy Jack is in the White House."

The bullets of a rifle fired from the sixth floor of a Dallas book depository dashed the hopes of Ireland, shattered the dreams of admiring citizens around the world, and placed an eradicable scar upon the history of our nation.

Two thousand years ago Christ also left home on a mission of mercy. He came to bring us the bread of life and the water of salvation and to assure us of His Father's love. While here, He was tempted without sinning, betrayed into calloused hands by one whom He had befriended, and murdered by enemies of His Father's cause.

The darkest hours of His ministry were the three days of incarceration in the iron house of death.

But unlike our boy Jack, whose remains lie beneath the flickering flame that marks his grave, our leader rose from the pit of death and ascended to the Father's throne where, adored by admiring angels, He now ministers to His human family.

He is our brother and because of Him we are joint heirs to heaven's riches. He is touched by our infirmities, thinking it "not robbery to be equal with God" and yet not ashamed to call us His brethren.

There, Son of God and Son of man, forever to retain His human identity, "He ever liveth to make intercession for [us]."

He is our Joseph in the courts of glory, our Barrister, our Umpire, our Lawyer, our Kinsman, our Benefactor, our Friend, our God of consequences, our Lord of forgiveness, and our Christ of eternal assurance.

Chapter 14

MARANATHA TOMORROW —KOINONIA TODAY!

"If a man love not the Lord Jesus Christ, let him be Anathema Maranatha"
(1 Cor. 16:22).

Someone once said with tongue in cheek that "it's very hard to prophesy, especially about the future."

That is true.

But I believe that it is almost as hard to gauge even the present. Experience in such matters tells us that it is rare for even analysts and editors to achieve a correct historical perspective upon their own times.

History has a way of mocking our evaluations of contemporary events. More often than not, the spotlight of retrospection (better known as hindsight) reveals that circumstances seemingly pivotal when being lived or witnessed were not that crucial after all.

Occasionally we do rightly recognize the historical import of an event. A national presidential election, a glowing advance in science or technology, or a major military victory by one of the world powers has obvious significance for tomorrow. On the other hand, many of history's watershed events were not so obvious when they occurred.

But in spite of our dismal record as seers, we are not safe unless we attempt to assess the impact of major trends and events.

It is crucial to the quality of tomorrow's society that we read carefully today's agenda, that we take time to thoughtfully examine the data now flashing on the charts of time.

It is not only important to know who we are but where we are in life's stream. I say all of this to introduce the following:

First, Oakwood College is now in the midst of a very real and meaningful transition. Of course there have been several other clearly identifiable transitions in our past. The move from manual training to a more liberal arts curriculum in 1911, to junior college status in 1917, to senior college status in 1943, and to full accreditation in 1961 all shaped who and what we are today.

Each of these moves led to the coming of age of Oakwood College as a bona fide and respected member of not only Adventist colleges but private Black colleges and higher education as a whole.

This transition shows up through the increased attention we are receiving in the media and in various educational organizations, by the membership that we hold in several prestigious scholastic bodies, by the quality of our faculty and curriculum, and, of course, by the fact of our burgeoning student body representing numerous states and countries. Our church now classifies us as one of its major schools—major in terms of institutional budget, faculty size, enrollment, and in the number and quality of our graduates.

Second, I wish to project that the trend will continue. Some members and church employees (both White and Black) question the maintenance of Black colleges in a day of integration de jure (by law), but I am convinced that the leaders of our church suffer no such illusion.

As far as I can see, Oakwood is in the budget to stay. Further, the rapid increase of Black Adventism (today one out of every five Adventists in America is Black), along with the renewed and enduring appreciation of Blacks for self-identity, added to the built-in support of our pastors (85 percent of whom are products of Oakwood), and the newfound respect that we have gained around the world all but guarantee our continued growth and expansion.

Additionally, the pressures of big-city life will continue to bring to Huntsville and vicinity families seeking relief from the concrete jungles of America.

The great migration northward is over.

True to Hansen's Law, which says that the third generation wishes to remember what the second generation sought to forget, the grandchildren of Blacks who migrated "up North" and "out West" are coming back to their Southern roots. The semirural South has become a haven for our disenchanted people. This reverse migration is a phenomenon in full swing. It consists of disillusioned Blacks who left "down South" only to discover that they had moved "up South," as King used to call the Northern states.

I wish to remind us that while growth and expansion are often desirable, and always exciting, they usually bring problems and perplexity.

Large numbers make for a diversified society.

A complex society inevitably separates its people into narrow groups of common interests—it produces specialized services and an atmosphere in which more people know a smaller percentage of the total population.

Institutionalization formalizes our responses and reduces our contacts. Suddenly we have more people to know and more places to go, but less time and less opportunity to become acquainted with one another. Sociologists discuss this phenomenon in terms of impersonalization, normlessness, and anomie.

The history of Rome in the ancient world and the whole course of Western civilization in modern times produces stark evidence of the social and spiritual ills accompanying these conditions.

To grow big is to depersonalize, to depersonalize is to dehumanize, and to dehumanize is to deny the very purpose of our existence.

Now, we probably have several options open to us at this time: 1. We can put a level on our enrollment, determining the "bounds of our habitation" and refusing to "lengthen our cords and enlarge our barns." 2. We can ignore the trend, take life as it comes, and depend upon our innate sense of unity and love to preserve at least some vestige of the "good ol' Oakwood spirit." 3. We can continue to allow our school to grow, meanwhile seeking to inaugurate plans calculated to preserve as much as possible the family feeling of the small college campus.

No matter which course we pursue, we will never be the same.

Those romanticists among us who long to see dozens of happy Black people laying down their hoes and gunnysacks a few hours before Friday sunset to shower and then file to vespers singing "Swing Low, Sweet Chariot" are probably in for frustration.

It might be well if we could, but in all probability we shall never fully recapture the essence of the former years when everybody knew each other's name and hometown, when the birth of a dairy calf was a big event, and going to town was a special treat.

However, may I hasten to add that in spite of the inescapable realities, we can neither please God nor adequately serve each other if we simply give up or become comfortable with creeping impersonalization.

The answer to our dilemma is, I believe, found in a term popular in New Testament theological circles. It is *koinonia*. New Testament writers, principally Luke, Paul, Peter, and John, use the word some 20 times to express various shades and nuances of the English word *community*.

In several New Testament passages it means "fellowship." Acts 2:42 says: "And they continued stedfastly in the apostles' doctrine and fellowship [*koinonia*], and in breaking of bread, and in prayers." Paul tells in Galatians 2:9 how "when James, Cephas, and John, who seemed to be pillars, perceived the grace that was given unto me, they gave to me and Barnabas the right hands of fellowship [koinonia]; that we should go unto the heathen." And 1 John 1:7 says, "But if we walk in the light, as he is in the light, we have fellowship [koinonia] one with another, and the blood of Jesus Christ his Son cleanseth us from all sin."

In other places koinonia means union or the oneness produced by the mystical bonds of Jesus' love. First Corinthians 10:16 reads: "The cup of blessing which we bless, is it not the communion [koinonia] of the blood of Christ? The bread which we break, is it not the communion [koinonia] of the body of Christ?" In still other places koinonia reflects sharing. Verse 6 of Paul's one-page letter to Philemon says: "That the communication of thy faith [koinonia] may become effectual by the acknowledging of every good thing which is in you in Christ Jesus."

What then is koinonia? It is the fellowship and unity and interdependence of those awaiting the second coming of Christ. Koinonia is having closer ties with you who are not my blood kin but who are fellow believers than I have with my blood relatives who are not believers. And it is accepting you and your idiosyncrasies and oddities as I need you to accept me with mine. When I take the cup or eat the bread or join hands with you in song and prayer, I acknowledge our common trust in the words of Jesus who 2,000 years ago promised to come again.

This promise of community gave birth to the New Testament greeting "Maranatha!" Early believers used it to remind each other again and again of the blessed hope.

Koinonia was their word for their relationship with each other until then. For them it was maranatha tomorrow, but koinonia today. Maranatha was the hope of the Advent, and koinonia their clinging together while anticipating this event.

And koinonia means that for us also. It is saying that in spite of all the time that has elapsed, in spite of the paucity of our numbers and the failures of our systems, in spite of all the centuries that have intervened, in spite of 2,000 years of disappointed expectation—we still believe.

We will believe even though we must die in that belief, as did the saints before us.

We choose to believe, not because we know no other theory, but because having heard the other theories, we have decided that the Christian hope makes the most sense. It strikes the warmest response in our hearts.

Thus we voluntarily bind ourselves together in this lifeboat of salvation where we have koinonia in hymns and prayers and the rituals of worship, and where we await His return in glory, or if He pleases, our call to rest.

If it be the former, we shall rejoice in visible redemption. But if the latter, we shall lie down in ripe old age in hope of the first resurrection.

And even if we do not see a ripe old age, we shall die reinforced by His Word and the warmth of our fellowship and say with the faithful of all ages, "I know that my redeemer liveth, and that he shall stand at the latter day upon the earth: and though after my skin worms destroy this body, yet in my flesh shall I see God" (Job 19:25, 26).

But *koinonia* is more than just believers associating together. It is concerned participation—participation in the rites of the community and participation in fraternal charity.

The King James translators have made Hebrews 13:16 to read: "But to do good and to communicate [*koinonia*] forget not: for with such sacrifices God is well pleased." *The New English Bible* has it: "Never forget to show kindness and to share what you have with others; for such are the sacrifices which God approves." Acts 4:32-35 clearly reveals that charity for the early believers had its basis in common ownership and a dedication of goods based upon need, not position or advantage.

The New English Bible reads: "The whole body of believers was united in heart and soul. Not a man of them claimed any of his possessions as his own, but everything was held in common, while the apostles bore witness with great power to the resurrection of the Lord Jesus. They were all held in high esteem; for they had never a needy person among them, because all who had property in land or houses sold it, brought the proceeds of the sale, and laid the money at the feet of the apostles; it was then distributed to any who stood in need."

Of course, our capitalist system makes ownership and private possessions almost mandatory. Few laity, or ministry for that matter, are willing to place all their deeds and funds in a common pool for general distribution to the poor and tuitionless. *Koinonia*, yes, but let's not be foolish—right?

Perhaps so, but one thing is certain: the more our community grows, the more we can expect the destitute and needy to gravitate among us. With continuing expansion, our *koinonia* opportunities are certain to increase, not lessen.

Hopefully, no one will go hungry in our midst and no stranger within our gates will suffer for lack of warmth or sustenance.

But I hear the questions asked, What about the freeloaders, the shysters who think the world owes them something? And what about the overly optimistic who had no business coming here in the first place? Don't we have to be careful about being duped in this *koinonia* business?

The answer is that misguided zealots who think that the church, the school, or even the denomination, owes them a living and who would take advantage of the *koinonia* principle will always be around.

We should separate insincerity from genuine need and respond accordingly.

Sometimes, believe it or not, for some people the best help is no help. But our most careful scrutiny notwithstanding, there is always the likelihood that some will eat and drink with us unworthily.

That, however, is not the greater danger. The greatest danger is that we who are well intentioned and even well supplied will become so skeptical, so suspicious, so afraid of being hurt, that our *koinonia* expressions will be stifled, or worse, lost.

Far better that we should freely love and freely share, even if we are occasionally deceived, than that we guarantee our not being hurt by repressing our *koinonia* impulses.

And while I am at it, let me zero in on one particular way in which *koinonia* can find expression in our midst. That is the area of financing or underwriting the Christian education of our youth.

Simply stated, no sincere young person should be denied a Christian education because of lack of funds.

When parents—and students when they are old enough—have done their best and still lack sufficient finances, it becomes the duty of the home church and even the home conference to come to their rescue.

Now that's *koinonia*.

Invoking *koinonia* will not get you past the business window next fall—that will take cash (the stuff with which we pay our bills).

Koinonia will not get you by your examinations and the quarter's end—that will take long hours of hard study, the just price of excellence.

Neither will *koinonia* save you from being put out of school or out of the church if your conduct requires it. If we are going to have a viable community and a healthy program there will be charges and collections, examinations and gradings, rules and regulations—and sanctions when they are broken.

But my plea to the entire community is that we not become so preoccupied with our business, our studies, our buildings, our research, and our social affairs that we lose sight of this precious virtue.

It is not too late to make up our minds. In spite of the inevitable by-products of our rapid growth, we still have a friendly campus. Students still seem genuinely happy to see each other every quarter—sometimes too happy—and the tears still flow freely each graduation when our seniors suddenly realize that—all of the strain notwithstanding—it was good to have been here.

We must not, however, be satisfied with a spirit of *koinonia* that just spontaneously happens. Instead, we must plan for its presence. Each of us must consciously build today so that tomorrow's Oakwood of 1,200 or 1,500 or 2,000 students—and that will happen if time lasts—shall remain focused in mission, unique in character, and warm in fellowship.

Can we preserve community in the period of exciting growth and dramatic transformation? Yes, we can, but it will not be by parroting the lifestyle of those who went before us here. We cannot return to those days. But we can by creative planning and aggressive implementation remain uniquely interlocked in purpose and community.

Magnetized not by tradition, ambition, nor even this marvelous movement itself, we are drawn here with our varied personalities and backgrounds to the cross of Jesus, where we can and must become one fellowship—one household of faith—completing not just our education but our likeness to Him as well. That is absolutely essential because our quality of *koinonia* is a primary factor in our quality of growth and preparation for service.

But then that changes our title, doesn't it? For if the completion of our mission depends upon the quality of our fraternity, in the final analysis it is not "Maranatha Tomorrow—*Koinonia* Today," but *"Koinonia* Today or Maranatha Never."

That is not a viable prospect. Our only choice, then, is to cling closely to our risen Lord, who alone makes Christian fellowship a reality and the Second Coming a reasonable hope.

God help us all to join hearts and hands in a solemn pledge to intimate relationship with Him and to increasing *koinonia*—Maranatha!

Chapter 15

FROM GOSHEN TO GLORY

"You shall live in the region of Goshen and be near me—you, your children and grandchildren, your flocks and herds, and all you have. I will provide for you there" (Gen. 45:10, 11, NIV).

he Story of Our Church records a dialogue between Rachel Oakes, Seventh Day Baptist, and Frederick Wheeler, a Methodist/Adventist minister, on a wintry day in 1844. The conversation went like this:

Oakes: "You remember, Elder Wheeler, that you said everyone who confesses Christ should obey all the commandments of God?"

Wheeler: "Yes."

Oakes: "I came near standing up in the meeting right then and saying something."

Wheeler: "I thought so. What did you have in mind to say?"

Oakes: "I wanted to tell you that you had better set that Communion table back and put the cloth over it, until you begin to keep the commandments of God."

That conversation was the beginning of the eventual merger of Sabbath observance with Adventism. By late 1844 nearly all of the charter members (about 40) of the Adventist Church of Washington, New Hampshire, had added the Sabbath to the judgment-hour message, and the Seventh-day Adventist Church was on its way.

And why? Why did God insist upon elevating the Sabbath to a prominent place in the work of the remnant church? Why does the prophet in *Early Writings* (p. 65) call the fourth commandment the greatest one of the Decalogue?

Why? For the very reasons God gave the Sabbath to us in the first place: as a memorial of His creative power, as a testimonial of His redemptive acts, as a bastion against idolatry, as a test of the loyalty of His people, as a sign of God's ownership, and, as our text indicates, especially as an aid to the health and welfare of the human race.

Consider how thoroughly the Sabbath fulfills this latter role. It does so by providing:

1. PHYSICAL REST

Coleridge is quoted as saying, "I feel as if God had, by giving the Sabbath, given fifty-two springs in the year" (quoted in *The Sabbath*, by James Gilfillan, p. 173). Isaac Taylor said, "I am prepared to affirm that, to the studious especially, and whether young or older, a Sabbath well spent—spent in happy exercises of the heart, devotional and domestic—. . . is the best of all means of refreshment to the mere intellect" (quoted in Gilfillan, p. 173). It is as if, says one Dr. Farre, "although the night apparently equalizes the circulation, yet it does not sufficiently restore its balance for the attainment of long life—hence one day in seven, by the bounty of Providence, is thrown in as a day of compensation to perfect by its repose the animal system" (quoted in Gilfillan, p. 174).

2. PERSONAL HYGIENE

The emphasis upon preparation that Friday holds is a weekly spur to cleanliness. Fridays demand clean closets, clean kitchens, clean bedrooms, clean clothes, clean cars, clean homes, clean persons. The stress upon physical hygiene and beauty as necessary conditions for Sabbathkeeping is a boon to health and an aid to longevity.

3. INTELLECTUAL REFRESHING

By bringing relief from the prolonged exertion of work and study the Sabbath refreshes and energizes our minds by bringing to us the grand and exalted themes of salvation. It stimulates and disciplines our intellectual faculties. It blesses our minds further by fostering ministry to others and fellowship with those of like faith—both of which bring joy and good cheer.

4. MORAL DEVELOPMENT

It was Blackstone who said, "A corruption of morals usually follows a profanation of the Sabbath" (quoted in Gilfillan, p. 194). And he was right, for one must have either appropriate rest or find some artificial means of sustaining oneself. The Sabbath provides the former, and as such delivers its devotees from intemperance that debases our moral powers. Further, Sabbathkeeping, by enjoining ethical duties upon our sons and our daughters, our menservants and our maidservants, and even the stranger within our gates, prescribes a high sense of moral responsibility for all within the sphere of its influence.

5. SYSTEMATIC BENEVOLENCE

In addition to the benefits already mentioned, the Sabbath teaches benevolence. First of all, having rested one day, we are more efficient and productive during the six days we labor. Consequently, our resources are more dependable, our storehouses more blessed. Second, by bringing our tithes and offerings each Sabbath, we develop a sense of mission and a generosity toward others that is both focused and consistent.

6. FAMILY SOLIDARITY

As a day of interaction and fellowship, the Sabbath provides cohesiveness and strength to the family unit. True, adherence to the fourth commandment is not as simple as it used to be, but the blessings to the obedient are no less real for us than for the chosen ones of antiquity. It is not only the complexity of our sociological situation that challenges us to remember the Sabbath—it is also our need for the blessings inherent in proper Sabbath observance. A brief review of God's instructions to us and our families is in order.

a. **Sabbath Preparation**: "All through the week we are to have the Sabbath in mind and be making preparation to keep it according to the commandment" (*Testimonies*, vol. 6, p. 353). "On Friday let the preparation for the Sabbath be completed. See that all the clothing is in readiness and that all the cooking is done. Let the boots be blacked and the baths be taken" (*ibid.*, p. 355). "We should jealously guard the edges of the Sabbath" (*ibid.*, p. 356). "Before the setting of the sun let all secular work be laid aside and all secular papers be put out of sight" (*ibid.*, p. 355). "Before the setting of the sun let the members of the family assemble to read God's Word, to sing and pray" (*ibid.*, p. 356).

b. **Sabbath Dress**: "Many need instruction as to how they should appear in the assembly for worship on the Sabbath. They are not to enter the presence of God in the common clothing worn during the week. All should have a special Sabbath suit, to be worn when attending service in God's house. . . . We are to be neat and trim, though without adornment. The children of God should be pure within and without" (*ibid.*, p. 355).

c. **Sabbath Rising**: "On Sabbath morning the family should be astir early. If they rise late, there is confusion and bustle in preparing for breakfast and Sabbath school. There is hurrying, jostling, and impatience. Thus unholy feelings come into the home. The Sabbath, thus desecrated, becomes a weariness, and its coming is dreaded rather than loved" (*ibid.*, p. 357).

d. **Sabbath Diet**: "We should not provide for the Sabbath a more liberal supply or a greater variety of food than for other days. Instead of this the food should be more simple, and less should be eaten, in order that the mind may be clear and vigorous to comprehend spiritual things. Overeating befogs the brain. The most precious words may be heard and not appreciated, because the mind is confused by an improper diet. By overeating on the Sabbath, many have done more than they think to dishonor God. . . . And let the meals, though simple, be palatable and attractive.

Provide something that will be regarded as a treat, something the family do not have every day" (*ibid.*, p. 357).

e. Sabbath Fellowship: "Communing together in regard to Christ will strengthen the soul for life's trials and conflicts. Never think that you can be Christians and yet withdraw yourselves within yourselves. Each one is a part of the great web of humanity, and the experience of each will be largely determined by the experience of his associates. . . . Fellowship with one another should make us glad. With such a hope as we have, why are not our hearts all aglow with the love of God?" (*ibid.*, p. 362).

f. Sabbath Conversation: "God requires not only that we refrain from physical labor upon the Sabbath, but that the mind be disciplined to dwell upon sacred themes. The fourth commandment is virtually transgressed by conversing upon worldly things or by engaging in light and trifling conversation" (*ibid.*, vol. 2, p. 703).

g. Sabbath Pleasure: "In order to keep the Sabbath holy, it is not necessary that we enclose ourselves in walls, shut away from the beautiful scenes of nature and from the free, invigorating air of heaven. . . . During a portion of the day, all should have an opportunity to be out of doors" (*ibid.*, p. 583).

"In pleasant weather let parents walk with their children in the fields and groves. Amid the beautiful things of nature tell them the reason for the institution of the Sabbath. Describe to them God's great work of creation. Tell them that when the earth came forth from His hand, it was holy and beautiful. Every flower, every shrub, every tree, answered the purpose of its Creator" (*ibid.*, vol. 6, p. 358).

h. Sabbath Rest: "None should feel at liberty to spend sanctified time in an unprofitable manner. It is displeasing to God for Sabbathkeepers to sleep during much of the Sabbath. They dishonor their Creator in so doing, and, by their example, say that the six days are too precious for them to spend in resting. They must make money, although it be by robbing themselves of needed sleep, which they make up by sleeping away holy time" (*ibid.*, vol. 2, p. 704). But while God does not expect us to reduce the Sabbath to a day of physical recuperation only, He does enjoin us that it is a day on which we may enjoy physical rest. "But as God ceased His labor of creating, and rested upon the Sabbath and blessed it, so man is to leave the occupations of his daily life and devote those sacred hours to healthful rest, to worship, and to holy deeds" (*My Life Today*, p. 231).

i. Sabbath Travel: "I fear that we often travel on this day when it might be avoided. . . . We should be more careful about traveling . . . on this day. . . . In order to reach the churches that need our help, . . . it may be necessary for us to travel on the Sabbath; but so far as possible we should secure our tickets and make all necessary arrangements on some other day. When starting on a journey we should make every possible effort to plan so as to avoid reaching our destination on the Sabbath" (*Testimonies*, vol. 6, pp. 359, 360).

Now, of course, Ellen White wrote most of this when life was quite different from what it is today. People did not have airplanes, comfortable showers, Piccadilly's and Morrison's and Country Kitchen restaurants, telephones or television, or much money to enjoy the meager comforts that were available.

Adventists were largely isolated on farms, lacking in education, bereft of property, and restricted in travel. They functioned within a hedge that effectively protected them from the inroads of society. But the hedge is no longer there—and even if it were, the scenery is vastly different.

We face decisions today that Ellen White never imagined. It is no longer possible to flip the pages of her books and find a precise parallel for the options that our present lifestyle suggests. But our contemporary environment notwithstanding, the strength of God's ancient mandate remains. There is no diminution in the sanctity of His holy day—no lessening of this vital command.

Are our houses in order *before* the sun sets? Is the carpet vacuumed, the furniture dusted? Is the grass cut, the car washed, the shoes shined, the buttons sewn on? Is the washing machine off, and if so, is the dryer off also? Are the blouses pressed? Is the hair washed? Is the food cooked? The beds made? The baths taken? Yes, the baths taken.

Now, before you judge me harshly, I'm all for showering on Sabbath morning. I do not take the prophetess' counsel against bathing on the Sabbath as an injunction against showering as we know it today. But the counsel does intend that when the sun sets on Friday evening, our bodies, as well as our surroundings, should be clean.

My proposition is that the legitimacy of showering *during* the Sabbath does not negate the necessity of showering *before* the Sabbath. It is both physically refreshing and spiritually symbolic. When we sit to sing "Day is dying in the west, heaven is touching earth with rest; wait and worship while the night sets her evening lamps alight through all the sky," we can sense that all of the week's cares and problems are now washed away, that we are meeting the King of the universe in fine style—refreshed, relaxed, satisfied, and expectant.

And what will happen when we regard this day as we should, when we seriously and consistently address the little foxes that gnaw at the vine of Sabbathkeeping?

According to Isaiah, when we engage in Sabbathkeeping properly, we shall delight ourselves in the Lord and He will cause us to ride upon the high places of the earth, and feed us with the heritage of Jacob, our father (Isa. 58:12-14).

Speaking on Jacob's heritage, *The SDA Bible Commentary*, volume 4, pages 27, 28 states: "God . . . provided them with every facility for becoming the greatest nation on the face of the earth. . . . It was His purpose to set them 'on high.' . . . They were to become a nation of intellectual geniuses, and feebleness of mind would eventually have been unknown among them. . . . The land would gradually be restored to Edenic fertility and beauty. . . . Pests and diseases, flood and drought, crop failure—all these would eventually disappear. . . . The Hebrew people were to acquire wisdom and skill in all 'cunning work,' that is, a high degree of inventive genius and ability as artisans, for the manufacture of all kinds of utensils and mechanical devices. Technical know-how would render products 'made in Israel' superior to all others."

Inspiration also tells us that the reason God sent them to the fertile land of Goshen (most likely in the northeast corner of Egypt) was that conditions there promoted the prosperity God intended. They were a shepherd people living in a land where "every shepherd was an abomination." But the very hostility they experienced in Egypt highlighted the miracle of their ascent to greatness that was climaxed in Solomon's day when the economy of the former "ragtag" people became the conversation piece of the ancient Near East.

But now I see another scene. I see a small minority hearing the gospel from the decks of the *Morning Star*. The sons and daughters of slaves are excited by the news of Christ's coming and are happy after 300 years of bondage to learn about not only a day of rest but an eternity of bliss. And I hear God decreeing that if "Ethiopia shall soon stretch out her hands," He will make this oppressed minority a crucial part of His remnant thrust. He'll use their musical ability, their preaching ability, their "soulfulness" as the cutting edge of the three angels' work.

And where will He let them spawn? What place will He appoint for the physical, intellectual, and spiritual development of this small but talented people? He'll lead them to the northeast corner of Alabama (in the fertile Tennessee Valley)—the home of the Klan and a bastion of racial animosity.

As with Israel in Egypt, He'll use the social oppression that engulfs them as evidence of His uplifting power. And He will give them 1,400 fruitful acres of ground. God will let them build dormitories and classrooms on the very plantation where their forefathers were sold as slaves. He will make this place the spawning ground for Black Seventh-day Adventism.

And if they obey His commandments and keep His Sabbaths, He will keep His promises. He will give them Jacob's heritage. They will be a nation of doctors and lawyers, and priests and kings. Their skin will be clearer, their grades higher, their acreage will yield more abundantly, their research will be more productive, and their graduates will build hundreds of churches and scores of schools and clinics. Nations will come to ask the secret of their power.

So that, not only will their children, unto the third and fourth generation, come back again and again to this place to be educated, but the stranger within their gates shall see in their programming the hand of God, whose commands are unalterable, whose promises are unbreakable, and before whom in eons to come, all God's children shall worship from one new moon to another and from one Sabbath to another—world without end!

Chapter 16

THEY WITHOUT US SHALL NOT BE MADE PERFECT

"And all these, while winning divine approval through their faith, did not receive the promised blessing; for God had in view something better for us, so that without us they would not be made perfect" (Heb. 11:39, 40, MLB).

The history of Adventism provides clear evidence of God's genuine concern for the place of Black Americans in His last-day redemption endeavors.

An analysis of our journey from 1844 shows that in the bringing together of believers from every nation, kindred, tongue, and people predicted in Revelation 14:6 as the cultural mix of Adventism, God Himself determined that "they without us should not be made perfect."

I wish to propose that we can best understand the phenomenon of our growth and participation by examining three major segments of our church's history: (1) 1844-1894, (2) 1894-1944, and (3) 1944 to present. I ask you now to join me in this study.

Since Adventism had its birth in the North some 20 years before slavery ended, we are not surprised that the Black presence was scarce among the early pioneers. In the first place, 95 percent of Blacks lived in the South in those days, and in the second place, Adventism, then as now, proclaimed a message best understood by those able to search the Scriptures, and most of the slaves were illiterate.

A second reason is that most of the free northern Blacks joined one of the several all-Black denominations—which came to be called the Independence movements—that already flourished in the North.

In spite these facts, however, pioneer Adventism was blessed with several Afro-American personalities who helped swell the midnight cry.

L. E. Froom, famous Adventist historian, writes:

"One of the unusual characters in the roster of Millerite preachers was a Colored minister, Charles Bowles (1810-1843). He was born in Boston, his father being an

African servant, and his mother the daughter of the celebrated American Colonel Morgan. . . . Though he often met with bitter opposition because of his color and the fact that he was preaching to large White congregations, he became a successful evangelist. His was the standard Millerite exposition of prophecy" (LeRoy Froom, *Prophetic Faith of Our Fathers*, vol. 4, p. 705).

Other early Blacks connected with this movement were John W. Lewis of Providence, Rhode Island, who too was a preacher, and William Foy, best remembered as the first Adventist to receive the gift of prophecy. The *Seventh-day Adventist Encyclopedia* describes Foy as a tall, light-skinned Colored man and eloquent speaker. Though a Millerite, when preaching he wore the robes of the Episcopal clergy. This source also states that his successor, Ellen White, regarded Foy's prophetic call as genuine.

O. O. Farnsworth, early Adventist historian, informs us further that Blacks were on board when the first SDA church organized in Washington, New Hampshire, in 1844. History is silent about their names, as well as of others who embraced the faith immediately after the 1844 experience.

However, in the middle 1870s the trail becomes distinct again. It was at this time that a trio of Whites (D. M. Canright, C. O. Taylor, and J. N. Loughborough) conducted separate but similar efforts to add Blacks to the fledgling denomination. As a result of their evangelistic efforts, Canright, who went to Kentucky in 1876; Taylor, who worked in Georgia in 1878; and Loughborough, who preached in Nevada in the same year, all wrote back to headquarters the good news of having baptized members of the Colored race.

Taylor was particularly thrilled to have baptized a Colored minister named Killen, and Loughborough was especially proud of a similar catch—a young man named C. M. Kinney.

In fact, J. O. Corliss, another early missionary to the South, reported to the General Conference in 1883 that the South contained 267 White and 20 Colored believers—thus roughly one out of 13 Southern Adventists was Black. Not a bad start!

During the 1880s the tempo accelerated, and a number of distinguished Black personalities accepted the truth. Sojourner Truth was baptized November 26, 1883, by Uriah Smith. Rosetta S. Douglass, daughter of the great Frederick Douglass, was baptized about the same time in Washington, D.C., and the first all-Black congregation was formed at Edgefield Junction, Tennessee, in 1883. That church service brought together the sum total of 10 cents during its first Sabbath collection. It was a small but significant beginning. In February 1889 a former slave by the name of A. Barry, as a result of reading the *Review and Herald,* became a Sabbathkeeper and evangelized Blacks in Louisville, Kentucky.

Shortly thereafter in June 1891 the Greensboro, North Carolina, church began. The Bowling Green, Kentucky, church started in September 1891, and the Nashville, Tennessee, church in 1894. The New Orleans, Louisiana, congregation was established in June 1892, and the Catchings, Texas, church in 1893. All of these, coupled with C. M. Kinney's ordination as the first Black pastor (October 1899), served as sure evidences of greater things to come and that even in our church's very beginnings, God had us in mind.

As this first 50-year segment of our church history ended, the organized body was itself solidifying its doctrinal positions and rapidly developing its institutional programs. The presses were rolling and the *Review and Herald, Signs of the Times,* and *Youth Instructor* were being printed. Missionaries left by the scores for overseas duty, and schools and hospitals sprang up around the world.

Thank God, we as Blacks were already affiliated in those foundation days—a small but faithful number. While our participation in leadership was still future, we were there, and it was clear that in spite of the paucity of our numbers, "They without us should not be made perfect."

The next major segment of Black Adventist history began in 1894, the year in which James Edson White, the son of the prophetess, built and launched the *Morning Star.* A year earlier James Edson had read a pamphlet entitled "Our Duty to the Colored People," written by his mother.

Inspired by Ellen White's concern for the neglected children of slavery, James Edson gathered about him a cadre of teachers and nurses, who, with the boat serving as a floating school and church, sailed down Lake Michigan onto the Mississippi River, where he docked at dozens of cities. Within the next 15 years, armed with two publications, *The Gospel Herald* and *The Gospel Premier,* as texts, James and his crew established 60 schools within six Southern states.

And speaking of schools, it was at the urging of Ellen White in 1895 that the church purchased 368 acres in northern Alabama for the sum of $6,700 and named the place Oakwood Industrial Training School. I am proud to report that one of the original 16 who comprised the first student body, Etta Littlejohn from Vicksburg, Mississippi, was my maternal grandmother. It was from the decks of the *Morning Star* that she first learned of the Sabbath.

But the most obviously portentous event in the 1890s was the mushrooming of Colored congregations—especially in the South: Lexington and Memphis in 1894;

Birmingham in 1895; Coriscana in 1896; Chattanooga and Charleston in 1898; and Orlando, Montgomery, and Winston Salem in 1899. And, as the twentieth century began, the phenomenon continued—Atlanta, Georgia, in 1900; Washington, D.C., and St. Louis in 1901; New York City and Kansas City, Kansas, in 1901; Kansas City, Missouri, in 1903; Mobile in 1904; Jacksonville, Florida, and Berkeley, California, in 1906; and Philadelphia and Los Angeles in 1908. The tide of the three angels' messages was rising to high proportions. Whereas in 1894 only some 50 Colored members lived in the entire United States, by 1900 there were 100, 1,000 by 1909, and 3,500 by 1918.

In 1883 the offering had totaled 10 cents at Edgefield Junction. Tithe had swollen to $50 by 1893 and $5,000 by 1900. By 1909 it was approximately $25,000. The General Conference session in 1918 saw Black membership total 3,500. What had been Oakwood Industrial School in 1896 had been renamed Oakwood Manual Training School in 1911 and Oakwood Junior College in 1917. We were growing within the church. The gospel story was finding a healthy reception among our people, and our response and development then in terms of membership, money, and budding organizational patterns again made it clear that "They without us should not be made perfect."

The period between the two world wars saw a number of events important to the continued development of Black Adventism. The first was a remarkable display of loyalty by its Black constituency when several of its leading ministers defected during the 1920s and the early 1930s. Chief among them were J. K. Humphrey of New York City and Charles and John Manns of Florida. They and a number of others left the Seventh-day Adventist Church because of disenchantment with what they saw as the group's racist posture. Their defection led to several independent Sabbatarian movements, some of which still exist, but the vast majority of Black members remained faithful in spite of obvious prejudice. Their love for God and truth superseded their concern, and Black churches continued to proliferate. There were 7,000 members in 1922; 12,000 in 1937; 17,000 by 1944.

Other major developments during these decades were the establishment of *Message* magazine in 1935, Riverside Hospital in 1936, and the coming of age of Oakwood as a senior college in 1943.

Fast on the heels of these events came the formation of regional (Black) conferences in 1944. By that time Black tithe income had grown to $511,000, and Black membership, which had been 3,500 in 1918, had now swollen to 17,000.

And with the development of Black conferences, Black Adventism took quantum leaps. Whereas there were 17,000 in 1944, there were 23,000 in 1950; 29,000 in 1955; 37,000 in 1960; 57,000 in 1965; 70,000 in 1970; 80,000 in 1973; 100,000 in 1977; 130,000 in 1983; and 193,000 in 1990. The 10 cents given in 1885 had become $18 million in 1977, $40 million by 1984, and $69 million in 1990. The 9 percent of American Adventism in 1944 became 20 percent in 1977 and 23 percent in 1985.

What more should I say, for time would fail me to tell of Abney and Allison, of Buckner and Branch, of Coopwood and Cox, of Dasent and Dillett, of Ewing and Edwards, of Ford and Follette, of Kimbrough and Knight, of Laurence and Lowe, of Manor and Moran, of Nunez and North, of Peters and Peterson, of Strachan and Scott, of Thomas and Troy, and of Warnick and Wagner.

All these and their colleagues through faith braved animosities, suffered prejudice, and sacrificed bravely to build schools. They constructed health centers and treatment rooms, wrote articles, and distributed books. Such men and women wandered about on bicycles and buses and lived in barns and tenement houses. Lied about and misunderstood, they often died at early ages. But all died in faith, not having received the promise. God, though, provided some better thing for us, "That they without us should not be made perfect."

Having this grand history and heritage, however, is not enough. The burning question is Where do we go from here? We are proud of the past, but we must also be stimulated by the present and challenged by the future.

And the question is Can we, in whose hands the torch has been placed, find victory in our day? Can we, building upon the foundations of our predecessors, contribute a quality of service sufficient for Pentecost? Or must this generation also lie down in death and leave to some succeeding group the thrill of the Apocalypse?

I firmly believe that Black Adventism is uniquely equipped to help the church reach ultimate victory, and that we can do so in the following ways. The primary contribution that we can make to our church is an infusion of the zeal and religiosity so common to our culture. It is no secret that Black people are highly expressive (unless spoiled by erudition), and more religiously inclined than most other groups—and for good reason.

First, we were already deeply religious when they found us in Africa. Our religious fervor, you might say, is genetically transmitted.

Second, our trials have driven us closer to Christ than we would have been had we not suffered the indignities of slavery, Jim Crow, and discrimination.

Being so long on the bottom of the sociological heap, we've had to depend upon Jesus for our sustenance. Ours is a living relationship—a daily bread experience—and that's the real reason our preaching is demonstrative and our testimonies so audible.

It is said of Christ while He was on earth that the poor heard Him gladly. The rich don't sense their need of divine assistance as easily as the poor. The advantaged don't have to pray for rent, and food, and clothing, as our parents did—and as we still do, in many cases.

In slavery we sang and prayed for deliverance. We cried for another world—a world of peace and rest and freedom.

After slavery we prayed for protection from the Klan and from injustice. Many thousands of mothers, scrubbing floors and washing clothes, watered their rags and brushes with the warm, briny tears of broken hearts, begging God for strength to keep on toiling.

We've come this far by faith, "leaning on the Lord," and that's why our forebears, bent with unbearable suffering, sang with deep meaning "Precious Lord, take my hand, lead me on, help me stand; I am tired, I am weak, I am worn; thru the storm, thru the night, lead me on to the light; take my hand, Precious Lord, lead me home."

However, the more affluent we become, the more educated and successful we are, the greater the danger that we shall lose that fervor, that we shall grow fat in the land of plenty and forget our God.

Isaiah cautions us to remain focused on "the rock whence ye are hewn, and to the hole of the pit whence ye are digged" (Isa. 51:1).

We must look beyond earthly prosperity to heavenly reward.

Rather than lose our zeal, we must allow it to serve as a catalyst to the other ethnic groups in our church. Our church needs a strong dose of Black enthusiasm. We have come to the kingdom for such a time as this. "They without us shall not be, *cannot be*, made perfect!"

The second contribution that we can make is a vivid demonstration of love and fraternity. One of Black America's most enviable traits is its magnanimity. In spite of all we've suffered, we find it hard to hate. I know of no other race as prone to forgiveness as ours. Despite oppression, we have remained, for the most part, a kind and openhearted people.

That doesn't mean we shouldn't stand up for our rights. There's a time to fight for freedom. Christians, too, are mandated to use legitimate weapons in obtaining release from social oppression. We too must work for justice in our communities, for better sanitation, better jobs, better education, recreation, housing, etc.

True, we'll never make a perfect society, but neither should we capitulate to evil. Each of us must by voice and by vote combat injustice—within and without the church.

But we must do so with a quality of love that evidences our Christlikeness, a love that binds us together here in our Jerusalem of fellowship but which at the same time establishes our place in the wider family of God—a love that allows us to fight for justice without and within the church as we remain always mindful that "they without us shall not be made perfect."

The third and perhaps most challenging contribution that I wish to propose is that of family solidarity. I realize that studies of family patterns are not usually kind to the Black community. In fact, if we are to believe them, our communities lead the way in illegitimacy, one-parent families, juvenile delinquency, joblessness, homelessness, and a lot of other characteristics of which we are not proud.

Our family reputation is not good. Oriental families, Jewish families, Indian families, Caucasian families, and others have, on the whole, a much healthier image.

But that is just the point! The very weakness associated with the broader Black American family makes the triumph of the gospel in our homes all the more impressive.

That gospel has redeemed us. The instructions of the Bible and the writings of Ellen White have delivered us from the clutches of superstition and ignorance that grip so many of our neighbors. Because of what the Bible has done for us and our children, we are living exhibits of the revolutionary power of the Word. We are proof that monogamy does work, that Christian education does pay, that endogamous marriage is right, and that those little red books—particularly *Child Guidance* and *The Adventist Home*—do make a difference. Our communities need this witness, and our church needs this testimony.

The evils of divorce and disease that inundate the larger society have brought great pain to the Adventist family system as well. We hear it at our college and academy campuses. One senses it in the alarming apostasy rate of our youth and in the escalating numbers of emotionally ill among our membership.

And that is where you and I come in. We, as no other group in America, know the value of family solidarity to group prosperity. It was destruction of valid family structures that initiated our descent into intellectual and moral poverty, and it was the restoration of family structures, sired by religious values, that has taken Black Seventh-day Adventists to new heights of social and economic strength.

And is this not a primary feature of the three angels' work? Did not Malachi promise that God would turn the hearts of the fathers to the children, and the children to the fathers, lest He smite the earth with a curse (Mal. 4:5, 6)? Did not John see the remnant keeping the commandments of God—most of which have direct reference to the home?

By observing the Sabbath we *have* ascended to the high places of the earth (Isa. 58:14). By returning tithe we have had the windows of heaven opened upon us (Mal. 3:10). By caring for our bodies we do enjoy superior health and longevity (3 John 2). We are redeemed not only spiritually but socially, and for that we thank God. And we can, if we will, use this miracle of grace to inspire our children, to invigorate our church, and to guide our witness as we individually and collectively go forward in contemporary fulfillment of God's design that "they without us shall not be made perfect."

Chapter 17

MAN, WHAT A CHANCE!

"And David put his hand in his bag, and took thence a stone, and slang it, and smote the Philistine in his forehead, that the stone sunk into his forehead; and he fell upon his face to the earth. So David prevailed over the Philistine with a sling and with a stone, and smote the Philistine, and slew him; but there was no sword in the hand of David" (1 Sam. 17:49, 50).

As battles go, it was a standoff of almost comical proportions. The armies of Israel and Philistia were hiding from each other behind trees and boulders on opposite sides of the valley of Sochoh.

Located about midway between Jerusalem and Gath, Sochoh was a natural amphitheater. For weeks the Israelites and the Philistines, camped on either side of this vale, had tested each other's resolve, called each other names, and dared each other to come out and fight. As we used to say when we were boys: "One was scared, and the other was glad, because he was scared too."

While no shots had been fired in this war of nerves, the psychological edge was definitely with the Philistines. Their leader was the giant Goliath, who had every day, without fail, presented himself in full view of both armies and loudly defied Israel and their God.

However, no Israelite warrior was foolish enough or courageous enough (depending upon how you view it) to take him on. Thus, they had been cowering in fear for 40 days when David, the kid brother of several of the soldiers in Saul's army, came along. His immediate mission was to bring food to his brothers—a package from home. You know how delightful that can be.

Sizing up the situation, David inquired, "What shall be done to the man who killeth this Philistine . . . ? for who is this uncircumcised Philistine, that he should defy the armies of the living God?" (1 Sam. 17:26). He was told that the man would receive great riches, the hand of the king's daughter, and free lodging for his father's household. No one guessed that he was thinking of doing this himself, and when he volunteered for the task, his brothers tried to dissuade him, telling him that he was too young, too small, and too inexperienced. It was too much of a chance. It was a chance but not a risk—it was a chance for the apparent weakest of Israel's number to demonstrate the miracle working power of God. A chance, yes, but what a chance, and David was equal to the challenge. Inspired and assured by a greater than human spirit, he filled his pouch with stones and ran out to meet Goliath and slew the mocking hero of the Philistines. When he had done so Israel exploded in joyful celebration and pursued and plundered their retreating enemy.

What we have here is a classic example of divine participation in human affairs—clear evidence of the superiority we enjoy when God is leading in our lives.

But this is more than a case of divine power overshadowing human strength.

The story of David and Goliath is really a microcosm of the church's protracted warfare against Satan and the enemies of righteousness.

And as I think of our young people today and their opportunity to assist the church in its victory, as I think of the privilege of being used on the battlefield of contemporary gospel endeavor, I am stirred to say what a glorious challenge, what a marvelous opportunity, what an unprecedented honor—man, what a chance!

At least three elements of David's story have potent parallels for our situation today. The first is *the extreme difficulty of the task.*

Goliath was not just another warrior—he was the biggest and the best and constituted the most formidable obstacle to an Israelite victory that Philistia could muster.

The church today faces its Goliath—the very immensity of our unfinished task. Matthew 24:14 states: "And this gospel of the kingdom shall be preached in all the world for a witness unto all nations; and then shall the end come." But between us and the lovely land of Canaan there remains this awesome obstacle—this Goliath—that has frustrated the people of God since 1844.

How great is our task? Well, 40 percent of the world can't read. Sixty percent is non-Christian, and our evangelism is being done by barely 5 percent of the 33 percent of humanity that calls itself Christian.

And it's getting harder all the time!

More and more people are being born—11,000 per day in the U.S. alone—than are being warned. We expect a world population of 8 billion by the year 2,000, and the burgeoning evils of intemperance, materialism, and pleasurism are more and more hardening the masses against religious truth.

Ours is a planet bathed in the flames of deadly tension and selfishness. It is a world gripped in the clutches of debilitating "isms"—evolutionism, atheism, nationalism, existentialism, scientism, individualism, Communism, hypnotism, spiritualism, separatism, socialism, relativism, individualism, situationalism, hedonism—in short, a world too profane, too mundane, too inhumane, too humanistic to respond to the logic and appeal of the Holy Spirit.

But then our God is no stranger to great odds. Again and again He has demonstrated His superiority over overwhelming forces. His ability to turn seeming defeat into victory reveals that our extremity is but His opportunity.

With Moses it was the Egyptians, the mountains, and the Red Sea; with Joshua it was the turbulent Jordan; with Elijah it was 450 mocking prophets of Baal; with Daniel it was the den of lions; with Paul it was sunken dungeons and sinking ships; with Jesus it was the raging seas, the hungry multitudes, the empty jugs; and with David it was Goliath.

With us today, it's a world wrapped in sin and sickness—caught up in the thrills and chills of its godless pursuits. It's a callous, careless, diseased generation of unscrupulous, misguided leaders and followers—but we must finish God's work.

Never has the world been this bad. But, God always hits better in the last of the ninth when the bases are loaded and the count is full, when it's fourth down and long. It looked bad for Joshua at Jericho; it looked bad for the Hebrew young men at the furnace; it looked bad for Esther and the Jews in Persia; it looked bad for David before Goliath; and it looked bad for Christ on the cross.

But that's all right. Go ahead, stack the deck. Give the devil a head start. God loves to win at the buzzer. He is a come-from-behind expert whose greatness is only magnified by the degree of difficulty the task presents. And just think, He uses us as instruments to accomplish His miracles—man, what a chance!

The second parallel we note is *the inadequacy of the instrument.*

Here God was using a mere teenager to thwart Goliath and his army. But then, sacred as well as secular history has often turned upon the heroic ministry of youthful heroes.

The Bible tells us of Daniel, Joash, Samuel, and Esther as well as David, here less than 20 years of age when leading nations.

And how about God's use of Joseph Wolff to proclaim the gospel at age 25? Ellen White relating visions at age 17? James White printing at 26? Anna Knight, a missionary in India at 27 years of age? Or F. L. Peterson teaching at Oakwood at 25?

But if none of those impresses you, remember the best example of all—Jesus Christ who by age 33 had been "manifest in the flesh, justified in the Spirit, seen of angels, preached unto the Gentiles, believed on in the world, and received up into glory" (1 Tim. 2:16). No wonder Paul said, "Let no man despise thy youth; but be thou an example of the believers, in word, in conversation, in charity, in spirit, in faith, in purity" (1 Tim. 4:12).

The prophet penned:

"The church is languishing for the help of young men who will bear a courageous testimony, who will with their ardent zeal stir up the sluggish energies of God's people, and so increase the power of the church in the world" (*Messages to Young People*, p. 25).

But note that David's youth was not his only handicap. He lacked not only experience as a soldier, but also the necessary equipment for battle. He faced Goliath not with mail and greaves but with a staff—a stick, if you please—a slingshot, and five stones.

Now, that's not much firepower with which to face Goliath. But God employs whatever talents we possess. He used Jephthah, a harlot's son; Gideon, the least of his father's tribe; Saul, who hid among the baggage; Joseph, the naive brother of Jacob's sons; and the unnamed lad with the five loaves and a few fish. Moses, when asked of God, "What is that in thine hand?" replied that it was only a rod. It *was* only a rod, but with it he divided the Red Sea, rained down plagues upon Egypt, halted the pestilence in the wilderness, brought water from the rock, and turned the tide of battles. God uses what one has.

What's in your hand? A little musical ability? Some skills at homemaking? A sunny personality? The gift of speech? teaching? science? writing? typing? power of persuasion? Whatever it is, give it to Jesus, and remember you don't have to be rated "most likely to succeed" in order to be a valuable instrument in the cause of God.

"Young men [and women] of ordinary ability, who give themselves wholly to God, who are uncorrupted by vice and impurity, will be successful, and will be enabled to do a great work for God" (*Messages to Young People*, p. 22).

Man, what a chance!

Finally, David's triumph is all the more memorable because of *the long-term consequences that it affected.* His deed was no isolated miracle. It was not only a watershed even in David's life; it was a pivotal event in Philistia's decline of military prowess and Israel's rise to international respect and authority. David's mission had been to deliver food to his brothers. His ultimate task was that of delivering Israel from a state of inertia and the launching of the career of one of the most powerful political figures of all time.

As David met and matched his challenge, so must we. This is our chance—our moment of truth.

David exercised three qualities of mind that should be part of our service today: 1. He was highly motivated—he literally ran toward Goliath (1 Sam. 17:48). 2. He refused to surrender his personality to another—he fought in his own armor (verses 38 and 39). 3. He was fortified for combat by the successes of prior battles—specifically, his victories over the lion and the bear (verses 34-37).

But then, are not high motivation, consecrated individuality, and courage born of confidence, traits common in many of yesterday's heroes?

Notice that Rebekah's servant ran from the well to tell of her encounter with Isaac's servant. Manoah's wife raced to her husband with the news of an encounter with the angel. Samuel hurried to Eli in response to God's midnight call. Cushi sped to David with the news of victory in battle. Elisha ran after Elijah as the prophet's mantle fell upon his shoulders. Mary and the other women ran from the sepulchre, having heard the good news of the Resurrection. Peter rushed to the tomb to verify their glad report. Philip ran to catch the Ethiopian's chariot. And Rhoda ran from the door to announce Peter's escape from jail.

Persons who are truly excited or motivated are not timid or hesitant. Great high dedication tolerates no neutrality, allows no hedging, encourages no indefiniteness. Those who are "eaten" by the "zeal" of the cause of God do not walk, stumble, or ease up on challenges—they run to their Goliaths in eager anticipation of whatever miracles are necessary for victory.

Notice too that we do not need to surrender individuality in His service. As David could not—would not—fit into Saul's armament or Barnabas in Paul's, or Apollos in Paul's, so none of God's instruments need mimic, idealize, or internalize the individuality of another. The God-given personality that each of us possesses provides a distinctive and needed expression for His cause.

"The younger worker must not become so wrapped up in the ideas and opinions of the one in whose charge he is placed, that he will forfeit his individuality. He must not lose his identity in the one who is instructing him, so that he dare not exercise his own judgment, but does what he is told, irrespective of his own understanding of what is right and wrong" (*Gospel Workers*, pp. 102, 103).

And it is also true that previous victories strengthen us for current conflicts. It is not tomorrow that we must be courageous—it is today. We must succeed against the little foxes that spoil the vine—in the common, ordinary skirmishes of life as we battle anger, pride, lust, appetite, and schedules. In the simple, everyday projects at home, at school, at church, and in the community, we develop the faith and muscle to take on larger tasks. As a result, the faithful do not retreat or cower before Philistian intruders. They do not hesitate to face even the Goliath that stands between them and their final reward.

Go On!

When Christ—our David—came to earth, sin had mocked the armies of heaven for 4,000 years. Lucifer, the champion of darkness, dared God to come down and fight. Century after century he exulted in his captivity of the human race. Then God sent His Son—His only Son—to bring us deliverance.

The Edenic promise said that He would crush the serpant's head and deliver His people. Isaiah reflected upon that and identified Him as our Champion, our "Wonderful, Counselor, The mighty God, The everlasting Father, The Prince of Peace" (Isa. 9:6).

And in "the fullness of the time" (Gal. 4:4) a voice was heard saying, Father, "a body hast thou prepared me" (Heb. 10:5). And that is when the celestial Warrior from the bosom of God became the Babe in the manger, soon to slay the dragon leader of darkness.

While the disciples cowered in fear, Christ won our release on Calvary. There He bared His chest to the thunderbolts of God's wrath against sin, and suffered as if He Himself had sinned. There He paid our debt and sealed the dragon's doom. And there He bore our sorrows and carried our griefs.

If He had not lived a sinless life as required, if He had not sacrificed His life as promised, if He had not taken up His life again as predicted, the plan of salvation would have failed. God would have lost a Son—and we would have lost eternity. But He won—the lamb prevailed over the serpent,

     the lion slew the dragon,
     What a God!
     What a victory,
     What a challenge,
     What an honor,
     What an opportunity,
     What a calling
     —man, what a chance!